THE YELLOW SHOE POETS

The YELLOW SHOE POETS

selected poems

1964-1999

edited by George Garrett

with a foreword by Fred Chappell

Louisiana State University Press
Baton Rouge

1999

08 07 06 05 04 03 02 01 00 99
5 4 3 2 1

Designer: Amanda McDonald Scallan
Typeface: AGaramond
Typesetter: Coghill Composition
Printer and binder: Thomson-Shore, Inc.

Library of Congress Cataloging-in-Publication Data

The yellow shoe poets : selected poems, 1964–1999 / edited by George
    Garrett ; with a foreword by Fred Chappell.
        p.   cm.
    ISBN 0-8071-2450-8 (cloth : alk. paper). — ISBN 0-8071-2451-6
    (paper : alk. paper)
      1. American poetry—20th century.   I. Garrett, George P., 1929–.
    PS615.Y37   1999
    811'.5408—dc21   99-27484
                                                         CIP

The paper in this book meets the guidelines for permanence and durability of the Committee on Production Guidelines
for Book Longevity of the Council on Library Resources. ♾

YELLOW SHOE POET

Right on time, a window open,
the pine table-top begins to release
memories like radium, glowing
to outgild anything that ever sang
in its branches awhile.

First week of June and pine pollen
is everywhere. It spins
a panhandler's dream around
the porchlight, and our cat
Blackie comes home
through the dark golden.

Once I thought I was here
to pass my kind on, a link
in the human trek, or to witness
and report the wren's arrival
across Homeric distances,

its tail-up verve around
the nesting box, how it chucks
last year's stuffing out
like a rout of fledglings, but
is this what I'm good for, to go
flatfooted through the pineys,
kicking up their ferocious yellow dust?

—*Brendan Galvin*

Contents

Foreword

Fred Chappell

Poets will count their successes in arcane ways. Great wealth generally will not accrue to them through sales of books, and they will never achieve the broad readership that a popular novelist can command. The honors they win—except for the Pulitzer Prize—are ones that few people have heard of, and the critics who acclaim their work are never household names.

So they look for reward first in the work itself, in the overcoming of dire obstacles only other poets would comprehend, in finding pleasure in the difficulties, in discovering a single line in which all the words and all the silences are irreplaceable and irreducible. Beyond the work, they look for refreshment of purpose from the comments of friends they must trust to be truthful and to the occasional alert anthologist who surprises by including in a collection not one of their worst efforts but one of their better. Every now and then a stranger's kind letter will light up a dim day the way a candleflame illumines the palm that shelters it from wind.

Another source of pride for the poet is in his or her publisher. It is a fine satisfaction to be able to proclaim silently, "My poems are brought into print by one of the most distinguished houses in the world." To find one's forthcoming title listed alongside that of a poet whose work one loves and admires produces a happiness almost aggressive: "There now, at least they can't take *that* away from me." The other poets in a publisher's list become brothers and sisters, and one shares, sometimes with a touch of envy perhaps, their joy at being prized and celebrated. Does not some of their honor rub off on oneself?

I count it highly fortunate that my poetry has always been published by Louisiana State University Press. It is with amazement that I look down their list of poetry volumes and find that I have read almost every one of them. I haven't admired them all equally and there are one or two I haven't admired in the least, but my first thought on seeing the titles together was, "If I were an editor, these are the books I would have published." As a longtime reviewer of poetry for newspapers and literary reviews and critical journals, I know that a list is as distinguished for its omissions as for its inclusions, and when I eye the table of contents here my heart leaps gladly to find certain names missing. I don't think this is mere meanness on my part; the truly worthy poets I happen not to like will find a house to take them in and bring them out. But the omission of certain poets from a list, especially if they have acquired some reputation, argues an editorial philosophy—and without such a philosophy a list will be undistinguished, however many famous names it parades.

I have never had the nerve to ask the folks at LSU Press what their editorial philosophy has been, but then I never felt I needed to. The list is a clear enough outline of their thought, as well as of their taste, and is apparent enough for all to read. Their say is not all that's involved, as each prospective volume must be submitted to outside readers, yet there is a consistency of tone, as well as of quality, that has produced a splendid list.

To all the editorial, production, publicity, and office staff in Baton Rouge we poets owe an immense debt. By their cheerful and tireless efforts they have given our work opportunity to be read and to be taken seriously. They have produced handsome volumes and presented them to whatever notice might be available. The rest was up to us, and this book you now hold in your hands allows you to decide if we—publisher and poet alike—have done well or not.

I think we have done well, but then I'm prejudiced—so wildly pleased to be included that at this moment all the world looks rosy.

Introduction

George Garrett

Following Fred Chappell, in life and in art, is to feel more than a little bit like (and here I steal a famous image from George Barker) a small dog running behind a brass band. He says the right things, the true things, the important things. And beyond that, the poems and the poets in this anthology will speak for themselves, tell their own story. Even so, Ole Fred, a courtly country boy if there ever was one, has graciously left me more than a little wiggle room for a brief introduction.

To begin, there is the history of it all. Hard as it may be to believe it, reader, from your stance at the tag end of this century, there was a time, and not so long ago in my own lifetime, when university presses as a matter of policy published very little poetry, a time when an anthology such as this one, representing some thirty-five years of the regular publication of contemporary poetry, would have been unimaginable. Back then, when I was a young beginner, some of the commercial publishing houses still felt some sort of vague obligation to publish some poetry. A few do, still, but not as many and not as much as then. And in those days university presses rarely, if ever, published poetry. The Yale Younger Poets Series, for first books, was in place; and other university presses (I remember some books from Princeton and Chicago and Rutgers among others) occasionally, for one exceptional reason or another, brought out a book of poems. It was something very unusual.

It is also true that those in the literary establishment, including most of the poets themselves, often took a dim view of poetry being published by university presses. It was the middle of the 1950s, and I remember well that it was considered bad form, one cut above publishing your poems by means of a "vanity press," to publish with a university press—even it there were a university press somewhere that would be willing to do such a thing. I remember (may I be personal?) that I was looking for a home for my second collection of poems and I was warned, by elders and mentors whom I admired, not to settle for a university press if there should be one that might somehow be interested. In fact, there was one—Frank Wardlaw's University of Texas Press, which had a connection with the well-endowed (now defunct) *Texas Quarterly.* That quarterly published "book supplements" as part of its elegant package; and soon enough they were publishing both fiction and poetry; these books in turn were brought out in hard cover by the University of Texas Press. The *Texas Quarterly* offered to bring out my book in that fashion and offered, not even as an advance against royalties, but rather in payment for the serial rights, the right to publish the poems as a book supplement, the lordly sum of $2,500. Disregarding all the advice of my elders and betters, I jumped at the chance.

What none of us knew then, though maybe the more prescient among us should at least have suspected, was that things were changing very quickly and completely. A year later, in 1959, the Wesleyan Poetry Series was put together and got under way. That was, at the outset, largely an accident. I was teaching at Wesleyan at the time and was witness to the whole affair. Wesleyan University sold off its scholastic publishing services, which included some fabulous cash cows like *My Weekly Reader,* for a great deal of money. The ever-watchful IRS suggested that in order to escape the slash-and-burn harvesting of the tax man, at least some of this wonderful windfall should be promptly spent on some worthy nonprofit enterprise. The publication of poetry seemed to the powers-that-be as good a way to be unprofitable as any other and a lot more fun.

Within a very short time, other university presses, for many different reasons, began to publish poetry on a more or less regular basis. One of these was the University of North Carolina Press, which established their Contemporary Poetry Series in 1961. I was the Poetry Editor for that series, working closely first with editor Howard Webber and then with a new, young editor—Leslie Phillabaum. We brought out some good books by good people, people like Mona Van Duyn, Lisel Mueller, Julia Randall, R. H. W. Dillard and David R. Slavitt among others. At the end of the 1960s that series up and died (and has not yet risen from the grave); but Leslie Phillabaum moved on to LSU, where they had already published some poetry under the encouragement and guidance of Miller Williams and John William Corrington. Williams later would become the first director of the University of Arkansas

Press, sponsored by the then-governor of Arkansas, William Jefferson Clinton, and would publish significant poetry there. At LSU, Phillabaum soon had a real poetry program, this one as it turned out, up and running. He also led the way by publishing outstanding original fiction as well, including the celebrated *A Confederacy of Dunces,* by John Kennedy Toole. As of this writing LSU no longer publishes original fiction, except for the international and annual Pegasus Prize; but their impact on the fiction scene is virtually undiminished, for the Press publishes Voices of the South, a series of trade paperback reprints of significant works of southern fiction. As of this writing, there are some 50 titles of the Voices of the South series in print.

So, in no time at all, in the blink of an eye, really, some university presses were now actively publishing poetry, and suddenly it was entirely respectable among the literati—poets were eager to submit to the university presses, all the more so since the big commercial publishers were rapidly fading out of the picture. And since those days—the late 1960s and early 1970s—LSU Press has been a major player, arguably *the* major player in the publication of contemporary American poetry. As it has worked out, there are other good and interesting poetry programs at university presses. Among them (and there are others) are Georgia, Alabama, Florida, South Carolina, Iowa, Ohio, Illinois, Arkansas, Carnegie Mellon, Pittsburgh, Johns Hopkins, and Wesleyan. But (have a look at the length and breadth of this anthology), the LSU program is at the top of any list you could care to make. Other presses have had their ups and downs, but the LSU list, richly various as it is, has maintained the highest level of excellence. If you want a clear sense of what has been happening in American poetry from the 1960s to the present, you can find that here.

Something else needs to be said about the surprising and changing literary scene from the 1950s to the present. Coterminous with the activity of the university presses, we in America have lived in the midst of a remarkable flowering of new poetry. Once upon a time a couple of generations ago, the poetry world, counting both writers and readers (often the same people), was a small one, composed of a few stars, a very few really. And ever since then it has been the business of those for whom poetry is a kind of business, professors and critics and the few commercial publishing houses still involved, to look for the new stars in the firmament. Sooner or later, in any given year, appears a familiar article asking the tedious academic question: where are the Eliots and Yeatses, the Wallace Stevenses and William Carlos Williamses, etc., of this age? The more adventurous of these pieces will then "discover" or "establish" some talented poet or two and name him or her or them the new kings of the mountain. The need to seek and find new stars is altogether understandable. And, not to be excessively cynical, it is ever so much easier to market accepted and recognized stars and to teach their works in fifty-minute classroom sessions, over quarters or semesters, than otherwise. In literary matters it seems that our gatekeepers and custodians prefer to pretend their world is both smaller and simpler than it really is or can be.

An accurate picture of our age tells quite another story. The second half of our century, at least in America, has witnessed a virtual uprising, a revolution in poetry, the likes of which has not been seen since the final decade of the rule and reign of Queen Elizabeth I. True, from our point of view, Shakespeare is the brightest star, the true North Star, of all our language. But consider the long roll of others who shared his time and world, and consider, as well, where he would stand without the plays, with only the sonnets and the narrative poems to celebrate his name. Maybe our own Shakespeare is also out there working in some popular form—as a filmmaker, perhaps. Somewhere or other, in an interview, the poet and translator Richard Howard has said of those who publish poetry today: "We are all minor poets." And that may indeed be the case, though the final judgment waits for another, later generation to be delivered. Meanwhile, on our own, as witness all the richness and diversity of this representative collection, we are in the midst of an exciting age of poetry, a time of many gifted poets, of many different kinds, ways, and means of making poems, and of a multitude of voices of all races and ages and cultures, many of which had not been heard of much, if at all, before our time.

And so here we are, thirty-five years and almost two hundred titles later, since the publication of *A Circle of Stone* by Miller Williams in 1964.

There are more than ninety poets on the LSU list. You will note that some of them, over the years, have published several titles with the Press, though there is no "stable" of "Yellow Shoe poets" nor any "school" other than excellence. There are some stars here, people who have been honored (or burdened, as the case may be) by national awards and recognition. Some others may not be so well known. All are worthy of your time and attention.

Finally, a word about the method and arrangement of this book. With the obvious exception of a few poets who have died and one or two we couldn't locate, the poets themselves selected the poem or poems, from their books published by the Press, to represent them. Poets are represented according to the number of titles they have on the list. Thus a poet with one book has one poem; a poet with two or three titles is represented by two poems; and a poet with four or more titles gets the maximum four poems.

(A "new and selected" collection counts as two titles.) With only a couple of exceptions, the poems are here published just as they were first published in the Press's books and have not been revised or updated.

What we are doing—poets, editor, all of us—is an act of celebration, celebrating this list and its publisher, and especially the director, Leslie Phillabaum, to whom we Yellow Shoe poets owe much and to whom all of us who care and are concerned about American poetry are so deeply beholden.

THE YELLOW SHOE POETS

Betty Adcock

DIGRESSION ON THE NUCLEAR AGE

In some difficult part of Africa, a termite tribe
builds elaborate tenements that might be called
cathedrals, were they for anything so terminal
as Milton's God. Who was it said
the perfect arch will aways separate
the civilized from the not? Never mind.
These creatures are quite blind and soft
and hard at labor chemically induced.
Beginning with a dish-like hollow, groups
of workers pile up earthen pellets.
A few such piles will reach a certain height;
fewer still, a just proximity.
That's when direction changes, or a change
directs: the correct two bands of laborers
will make their towers bow toward each other.
Like saved and savior, they will meet in air.
It is unambiguously an arch and it will serve,
among the others rising and the waste,
an arch's purposes. Experts are sure
a specific moment comes when the very structure
triggers the response that will perfect it.

I've got this far and don't know what
termites can be made to mean. Or this poem:
a joke, a play on arrogance, nothing
but language? Untranslated, the world gets on
with dark, flawless constructions rising,
rising even where we think we are. And think
how we must hope convergences will fail this time,
that whatever it is we're working on won't work.

AT THE AGE WHEN YOU
GET BAD NEWS

Letting go of the future
is like this: trying to fit
back into the camera's aperture
before it closed that little square of time.
In this snapshot, I am fifteen,
all opening before me. I squint hard
against such brightness; perhaps I feared
the shutter's snicker.

Memory adds to what's outside the frame—
that fence, all rough-barked wood,
where my grandfather hung the dead
rattlesnake that wouldn't stay dead.
That fence, and the field beyond it
overgrown, one slightly agitated cow
heading for a shade tree.

But all that's beyond the picture's reach.
Here I am, feckless and posing.
My father stands beside me with his stick.
He's looking down so there's no face to him,
just hat with the brim turned down.
I'm wearing the sweater of pale lavender
that seemed made for someone prettier,
like the deep purple skirt
of corduroy soft as velvet.
It's all gray in this black-and-white,
the colors I'll get where I'm going.

In the picture I'm sitting on my heels
hugging the cur named Red
my father kept for squirrels,
and some of those in the out-of-focus trees
making the big dog's head begin its easy
swing toward joy, just as I am turning already
toward the path to this day two thousand miles away

that has brought me another death
and this kind of travel—
I do manage to get there before the picture,
where it's darker than it ever gets
until you've traveled afterward yourself.
Nobody's looked yet through the finder,
the lens not set, boundaries of white
paper not yet interrupting a translated sun.
I don't know what's going to happen
all over again at the speed of light:
the trees, my father, the blank sweater,
that dog starting to run.

THE KINDS OF SLEEP

First there's the one in which all the children
your parents wanted you to be are chosen.
The sheep from the goats they said in Sunday school.
You remember judgment: it's cool as blue marble,
quiet as a hospital. All the others
have been led to honeyed pastures—
is that it? Anyhow, you are the only goat,
stuck in a stone place with your own sad smell.
Nobody cares if you wake up.

You may sleep to believe in ink.
It seems to be ink but there's more of it,
viscid, a blot that will cover everything.
And with no words in it, nothing but black.
You have been made responsible. So you push,
you push to save whatever you can from the dark.
It seeps through your fingers, gets worse.
For a whole mysterious night you have to be Sisyphus
lacking a stone, wrestling an angel of pitch,
the black in *black plague,* the perfect

coherence of floodwaters.
You give your right arm for an edge.

Then there's the walking sleep.
It's dark, but somehow the right house
assembles itself under your feet.
You step into air and it's there,
the kitchen with the pie-safe and pictures
of white roosters, the dining room window
framing oak trees and the fishpond;
the rooms with their sentinel fireplaces
coming to be in your footfall.
A thorntree of fear grows in your throat
when you remember the house
will end, used up, at the porch rail
beyond which the rest of your life
is creating you step by step.

Last is the sleep with flowers
and the golden fishes you have come to feed,
a child with raw oatmeal in your pocket,
zinnias in your leftover Easter basket.
This is the sweet one. You have forgotten
everything except morning where it is always morning,
and your ignorance surrounding you with green,
with presence, with your body that can merge,
like the pomegranate on its tree by the fence,
with light. All that you never want to know
has gone, has not come. You slip off the last
porch step into the dewy grass, the path
to the pool where goldfish break black water
that folds again into night above their lanterns.
The goat in the pasture lends you his eye of surprise
as the world fails and you step onto white
     bedsheet   feathers   paper   snow
on which you will lie down, not even flailing
an angel shape, not breathing your small tune, not
writing your name.

TO SYLVIA, GROWN DAUGHTER

You who loved so much the creek mud
and the green-shaded woods, all many-
legged moving things, all small hiding
flowers—so like yourself then—
now you are this tall someone
and bright as a fire. Dear lantern!
But listen:

lit with fallen apples and plain grass,
with salamander and birdfeather,
with candles of spring pine,
the old rooms will have waited
the way a forgotten house waits at the edge
of a snapshot you hardly meant to take.
The place has its own moon
and no noise but the cricket's skinny one.

You may enter by the door of what is not yet,
as you did before. Or by the new door
of what has been taken from you.
Pain will let you in, or fury. Ordinary
love will let you in, or any dying.
No key is too odd, no reason too far away.

It is only the house of your first name
that belongs also to the skyful of branches,
to dove, treefrog, and milkweed,
those who begin again.
I say this because it is so simple.
I tell you because it is anyone's,
and because the likeness may be torn
by now. And you may not know.

CITIES & EMPIRES

The secret is not to move, the lady said,
But sometimes you can turn your head away
For a minute, then back, as you do to really watch
A sunset, and you do this several times, and then
You can feel the dark on your eyes like a cold cloth.

That's how it was, she said. When the soldiers went by—
Straight lines of them, like holes in a cribbage board;
Men no older than my boy they caused to vanish—
I stood, but stared at nothing. Others told me
A haze of apple petals fell about them slowly.

And when I looked back, they were gone. The road
Was empty, save for cars with blackened seats,
And a body or two. It was comforting, that quiet,
For I was thinking of coffee, I was thinking
Of holding my hands around a cup of coffee.

You must do it, after all, she said—your eating,
Washing, sleeping, suffering. The mind has little rooms
It rents out to the body, and at times
You go there, no one follows you, the shades are drawn,
Dust falls like fingers from each one you touch.

THE PEOPLE THROUGH THE
TRAIN WINDOW

All we'll ever know of them are the lights
of their houses in the late evening winter,

and that their lives are intertwined as ours,
as lonely as a Scott Fitzgerald story.

Born to rush out on the earth and die,
how strangely we behave, as if it were not true
that there will be old gravestones up above our bodies,
and our children will be thinking of us sometime.

How else can I say it? We will die
and not come back, not ever, not return
to mystic restaurants and words we've spoken softly,
strokings, glances, and confessions, and

the seasons of this lovely planet will take no
notice of our vanishing; my hands
will lie as silently as yours; the wind
above the planet will not touch your eyes,

nor, within a hundred years, one face
of those within the houses with the lighted rooms.
Can we imagine that? All dead, all dead,
all of us all dead, who never lived enough.

Good Lord, the carpe diem poets in their graves
were so right that it makes me tremble when
I think of falling into love, and out, and in again,
or listen to Jim Croce in his Creole voice.

Seize the day, oh seize the day, oh seize
your life with every tendon, every thought you have;
the moonlight hits the window, and the stars
have always gone this crazy in their crazy sky.

AUCTION

Some things bring nothing. Later there will be
a bonfire of palm-worn plow handles.
But a doll, pallid—china hands fractured—
brings fifteen dollars.
                          His bed they have hauled
out, the covers still on it, an old man's
nest of tangled flannel. I think he has
no daughters to know what must not be
sold. His late wife's dressing table gives up
its confused vanities: snaggletooth combs,
the warbled wire of hairpins, a lipstick,
a faint layer of blush over all. The sun-
shocked mirror denies this face, waves my hair,
widens my eyes, until I cannot see
the resemblance. Is this how she saw
herself? And over her shoulder the fields,
falling away from the house, steep with
distortion? Under her crushed narcissus,
the varicose wake of a mole heaves
as if the vagrant dead—grown bolder—rise,
thick palms bared for this shallow, movable darkness.

THE FAILURE OF SOUTHERN
REPRESENTATION

I

Sunlight's impasto on brightleaf has not yet
Curled wet-lipped, no moccasin-caduceus on cypress has
Slithered in succulent gesture. Unrepresentable
Vacancies blotch the historical record, as invisibly
The dead bitch bares teeth in the mud ditch.
Within the undetermined census of these pines,
Beside these sobbings, lynchings, cries extracted like
Turpentine from resin, no palette has tar enough.
Under even this present burn of noon no cadmium
Or zinc is vivid as the life, the art is choked.
Expressways paved over the past cannot express,
Though sheet metal signs rise yellow as tobacco,
Are veined by collisions and hurricanes. Shopping centers
With their tourist pastels are dumb as tombs in this land
Still furious with its phantoms. This surface can be neither
Painted nor spoken, no oxymoronic pigment is mixed
To render livid noon as coal midnight. Footsoldiers'
Shove and charge imitated by commercial assault
Cannot cohere into this silence of vista
Still as the coral shelf under green fathoms.

II

Memorial heads outside the libraries erode
And disassemble, tar-dark patches like spots of shame
Inhabiting the marble. Names implanted in this terrain—
Civil War heroes, progenitors of civic virtue—fall ill
As I look. Limestone flakes blow away in wind
Like flesh dropping in leprosy. Yet this also is
Inaccurate, hypothetical. The columned, white plantation

Invents itself on front porches now wholly vanished,
Inherited from fictitious aunts, fabulous uncles.
Accents which deep in their vowels have
Never given up the slaves come back
To haunt us, a chorus, a convention of narration.

III

Music. Music more probably represents, if we admit
That the fall of moonlight on tidal rivers cannot
Be heard or suggested, that negro spirituals,
Condensed into an atmosphere of pain,
Erode the stelae in Confederate cemeteries
To namelessness, to silence. That now we number
The thud of boxes from eighteen-wheelers
At docks in Atlanta, the diesel thug thug,
The tin clang of dimes buying polyester scarves,
As glass tones from stereos strike tin
Horizons, where barns are pinned to burn
In the unvoiced uproar of glare.

FORESEEING THE JOURNEY

The fan inhales one continuous breath: through
This upstairs room I am lying awake in, foreseeing the journey.
This creek, this street, this one row of houses, diagram Town.
As simple as the world. As air and the light. Old birthplace.
Tomorrow we'll go with the current, canoe around snags—
As I guide my son through the thicket of childhood—
Past moccasins uglier than the Biblical serpent.
Passion-flowers as in Rousseau's jungles.

This four-bladed beating, as of great hawks crossed,
Sucks moths from their flight, with light's
Exhalation, draws foil-glint wings from the corn.
Its rumble surrounds me. Our bungalow lifts off, zeppelin
With roof, shadow more angled than a biplane bomber.

I seem Huck Finn visiting a house on the flood.
Books from around me hover their pages. With Zane Grey
And Edgar Rice Burroughs, presents bobbing up like helium
In the attic—my Christmas models in a loose formation—
I fly in the flock of these presences, owls with the heads
Of dead relatives, the photograph of my mother's brothers
Sailing in the ghost wind, until the huge cry they feel
Becomes one with the wailing of the fan,
This rest what I can do and no more fear.

Almon who told me the Cyclops' blinding
Looks so beautiful there, delicate of feature, shy
With sister, ignorant of the years of high school teaching,
The loneliness to come. But not consumed
By my mother's weeping, for all who have died,
Her father Mercer's fall under his buggy,
I fly in this house and its history
As in Lord Greystoke's plane above the trees.
Would any of us be born into the world
If we had it to do over?
Through this sleep of the unborn and of spirits
The propeller tom-toms a message.

The attic fan in this window, ill-designed,
Dangerous, great blades unshielded, drive belt
Exposed to the unwary night walker,
Put in by my father in jack-leg fashion
Like everything down east, by him who lost
His fingers to an air compressor belt,
Seems the risk of all living. I'm flying too high
But in the dawn light chill I reach down
To find a blanket green as leaves.
I pull up the jungle over my body.

A WILSON COUNTY FARMER

The mercury-vapor yard light on a pole
    comes on automatically at dusk, triggered

it seems by the television's phosphorescent glow in
    the front room, seen icongruously through those
sashes and panes from just after the Civil War.
    The middle-aged farmer standing in shadow of this
unnatural light before his packhouse, still smoking
    a Lucky, just a few in any day now, sees
heads of his wife and daughter-in-law through the
    window, and the grandson's occasional, ball-quick
passage through color, and thinks maybe he has survived
    too long. Life is easier, maybe, with MH-30
to inhibit suckers, the tractor-drawn harvesters,
    where croppers ride close to the ground, breaking
off leaves, clipping them into the reeled chains. But hands
    are undependable, and without his blood kin,
a man couldn't hardly be sure of a harvest crew.
    Some use the migrants, hard-working, ignorant
of the ways of tobacco. With the quotas, the declining
    prices, every day more news about cancer, this man
who learned tobacco from his father, who himself couldn't
    read and write, looks far across at red Antares
over the swamp woods there beyond the highway, not knowing
    what star he is seeing, and feels his station in this
place lit by blue light and T.V. as odd and as lonely.

BARBECUE SERVICE

I have sought the elusive aroma
Around outlying cornfields, turned corners
Near the site of a Civil War surrender.
The transformation may take place
At a pit no wider than a grave,
Behind a single family's barn.
These weathered ministers
Preside with the simplest of elements:
Vinegar and pepper, split pig and fire.

Underneath a glistening mountain in air,
Something is converted to a savor: the pig
Flesh purified by far atmosphere.
Like the slick-sided sensation from last summer,
A fish pulled quick from a creek
By a boy. Like breasts in a motel
With whiskey and twilight
Now a blue smoke in memory.
This smolder draws the soul of our longing.

I want to see all the old home folks,
Ones who may not last another year.
We will rock on porches like chapels
And not say anything, their faces
Impenetrable as different barks of trees.
After the brother who drank has been buried,
The graveplot stunned by sun
In the woods,
We men still living pass the bottle.
We barbecue pigs.
The tin-roofed sheds with embers
Are smoking their blue sacrifice
Across Carolina.

Jimmy Santiago Baca

THE COUNTY JAIL

Men late at night cook coffee in rusty cans,
just like in the hills, like in their childhoods,
without rules or guidance or authority, their fathers
dead or wild as gypsies,
their mothers going down for five dollars.
These are the men who surface at night,
The sons of faceless parents,
the sons of brutal days dripping blood,
the men whose faces emerge from shadows,
from bars,
and they join in circles and squat on haunches,
share smokes, and talk of who knows who,
what towns they passed through;
while flames jump under the coffee can,
you see new faces and old ones,
the young eyes scared and the old eyes
tarnished like peeling boat hulls,
like wild creatures they meet,
with a sixth sense inside of them, to tell them
who's real and who's the game;
and their thoughts are hard as wisdom teeth,
biting into each new eye,
that shows itself around the fire.

The coffee is poured steaming hot into cups,
and the men slowly sip.
Shower stalls drip bleakly in the dark,
and the smell of dumb metal is inflamed
with the acrid silence, and once in a while,
a car horn will sound from outside the windows,

and the man with only a cheek illuminated by the fire,
the rest of his face drenched in shadows,
will get up and leave the circle,
return to his bunk.

Gerald Barrax

SAINTHOOD

Dying is the easiest thing they have to do,
Their only way to campaign for canonization—
Accepting or seducing arrows and fire,
Abandoning the flesh and its mortal debt.

Thomas à Becket had good PR and made
Saint in three years, Assisi in only two;
Others must wait decades, centuries, to work
The required number of miracles.

Martyrs, come bring your postulators and devils'
Advocates, crowd quietly into this room
And bear witness to what I live to do:

An hour I've battled this recalcitrant child,
This relic of my flesh you see in my arms,
Before she would be rocked and sung to sleep.

THE GUILT

He made himself her compost heap, and hoped
Something old or something new would grow
Where he kept the guilt always in the best light
For her tending, fertilized with bile and bonemeal
Ashes shaken through the grate in his heart.
She used her privilege of a good woman done wrong
And opened him up at will to nurse and prune
It, until the habit of their make-do lives
One day lulled them offguard into a casual quarrel,

And she turned at bay with her cri de coeur,
"I will never forgive you, never." He set his face
To muffle its shout of deliverance
When his seahorse womb aborted the misshapen thing
And, midwife to himself, he became a something new.

XEROX

The original man lies down to be copied
face down on glass. He thinks what it is
to be other than he was, while the pilot light
goes garnet, a salamander's eye
blinks in the camera's cave, green burns like the skin
of the water seen by a surfacing swimmer:
and the moving and shaking begin.

What must it be, to be many? thinks the singular
man. Underneath, in the banked fluorescence, the rollers
are ready. A tarpaulin falls. A humming of flanges
arises, a sound like rail meeting rail
when power slams out of the fuses. A wick explodes
in the gases—and under the whole of his length
the eye of the holocaust passes.

And all that was lonely, essential, unique
as a fingerprint, is doubled. Substance and essence,
the mirror and the figure that printed the mirror,
the deluge that blackened creation and the hovering pigeon
with the leaf's taste in its beak,
are joined. The indivisible sleeper is troubled:
What does it mean to be legion?

he cries in the hell of the copied. The rapists, the lovers,
the stealers of blessings, the corrupt and derivative
devils, whirl over the vacant emulsion.
The comedian peers from the brink and unsteadily copies
its laughter. The agonist prints its convulsion.
Like turns to like, while the seminal man on the glass
stares at his semblance and calls from the pit of the ink:

Forgive our duplicity. We are human
and heterogeneous. Give us our imitations!
Heart copies heart with a valentine's
arrows and laces. The Athenian dream and the adulterers paired
in the storm tell us the mirrors are misted. The whole of our art
is to double our witness, and wait. And the original man on the plate
stands and steps down, unassisted.

THE ORANGE TREE

To be
intact and unseen,
like the orange's scent
in the orange tree:

a pod of aroma
on the orange's ogive of green
or a phosphorous voice
in the storm of the forge and the hammer:

to climb up a ladder of leaven
and salt, and work in the lump
of the mass, upward and down
in the volatile oils of a wilderness heaven:

to sleep, like the karat,
in the void of the jeweler's glass,
yet strike with the weight of the diamond—
perhaps that is to live in the spirit.

So the orange tree
waits on its stump as the wood of its armature
multiplies: first, the branch, then the twig in the thicket
of leafage, then the sunburst of white in the leaves, the odor's epiphany.

All burns with a mineral
heat, all hones an invisible edge on the noonday, while the orange's scent
speaks from the tree in the tree to declare what the holocaust meant:
to be minimal,

minimal: to diminish excess, to pare it
as a child pares an orange, moving the knife through the peel
in a spiral's unbroken descent, till only the orange's sweat,
a bead of acidulous essence, divides the rind from the steel:

perhaps that is to live in the spirit.

Catharine Savage Brosman

THE BOOKSELLER

Until I die, I shall abide by books—
feeling the leather and the gilded spine,
running my thumb along the rippled edge,
sensing the musty cloth, the wormy page,
the odor of a chest or rooms untended
where a distant heir one day divined
a windfall for his bank account, and called
on me. Here, watch your step; I cannot

see, but my companion says that books
have almost filled the hallway, overflowed
the bedroom, where I feel their presence
at night among my dreams.—Will you have
some tea and scones, or else a hot cross
bun, to mark the season? Yes, all London
bustles here on Oxford Street, and I suppose
I need the sense that others are about;

but what we know most keenly is desire,
and in desire I know the darkness, not
the life I hear but that which I imagine—
the way you, reading of the Trojan War
or the Crusades, perhaps, are startled
by the telephone, thinking of Helen's face
instead, of Hector's body pulled behind
the wheels of arrogance. Tamer of horses

I can never be—but rider of another world
informed by paper—and, for me, in tongues
beneath my fingertips. To sell, of course,
is necessary, and I thank you; but I need
to feel beside me, too, this field of words

aflame, where blinded poets make the Sirens
sing, and I can almost glimpse the light,
the dazzling seascape that Odysseus sailed.

ASPARAGUS

Sweet stalks!—found at a French Market
stall in their greengrocer's bundle,
half-disguised by lettuces and chards,
a bit of roseate root still visible,
and crowned in forest fronds—now cooked
(as if intended from eternity for butter

or a hollandaise), await our delectation.
Laureates of salad, lances for a royal
plate, acanthus of the dinner table—all
the images you wish, and nothing more.
For they are either only a phenomenon,
an indicator of the world—a vegetable—

or they are of the mind, a verdant poem;
if so, I thank you, I'll not countenance
that talk of symbols and of Dr. Freud.
Let him dream on in slumber undisturbed,
see monsters coupling if it pleases him,
or virgins in Vienna panting in pursuit

of fleet phantasmagoric phallic forms:
these grainy-tipped and handsome spears
suggesting still a ferny perfume, fresh
as from a kitchen garden, offer no one's
fantasies, but sun and rain and mineral
transformed, a celebration of the earth

made edible and toothsome for our flesh,
by which we realize in bodies an idea,

like music played on carcasses of wood
and string, as world and image coalesce,
the soul of feeling magnified in sound
and vibrating to heaven's leafy vault.

Paula Closson Buck

THE ERRAND

Between departing and the loaf of bread,
between your door
        and the plague of white moths the mini-mart suffered
last summer, you know the other man waits.
His shadow is patient among the hedgerows.

                        If you loved him, just a little,
you became a little grotesque, like the figures your husband
    sketches in coal,
their tiny heads spoiling the big, beautiful thumbs.
                        Somehow, you too
have run afoul of beauty, though it was everywhere,
        bringing you gifts.
And though your child's hair is silken
                            at nighttime to your touch,
you may never arrive at the well-lit stoop, paper bag in hand.
Evening's slow candor receives you again. From among

the day's artifacts, a geranium has plucked something red.
            In the scroll and smudge of dying light,
sustained like the humor of the bereft,

things hold their shapes.
            You are beginning to see the human face
as the only form of righteousness.

    Forehead when the hair's smoothed back.
Carthusian meeting of nose
                    with upper lip. What remains
of stories and vows,
        stacked below in the mouth's deep catacomb.

Kathryn Stripling Byer

WEEP-WILLOW

At night she watched the road
and sang. I'd sigh and settle on the floor
beside her. One song led
to one more song. Some unquiet grave.
A bed of stone. The ship that spun round
three times 'ere it sank,
near ninety verses full of grief.
She sang sad all night long

and smiled, as if she dared me
shed a tear. Sweet Lizzie Creek swung low
along the rocks, and dried beans rattled
in the wind. Sometimes her black dog howled
at fox or bear, but she'd not stop,
no, not for God Himself, not even if He came
astride a fine white horse and bore the Crown
of Glory in His hands. The dark was all
she had. And sometimes moonlight
on the ceaseless water. "Fill my cup,"

she'd say, and sip May moonshine
till her voice came back as strong as bullfrogs
in the sally grass. You whippoorwills
keep silent, and you lonesome owls go haunt
another woman's darkest hours. Clear,

clear back I hear her singing me to sleep.
"Come down," she trolls,
"Come down among the willow
shade and weep, you fair
and tender ladies left to lie alone,

the sheets so cold,
the nights so long."

MOUNTAIN TIME

News travels slowly up here
in the mountains, our narrow
roads twisting for days, maybe years,
till we get where we're going,
if we ever do. Even if some lonesome message
should make it through Deep Gap
or the fastness of Thunderhead, we're not obliged
to believe it's true, are we? Consider
the famous poet, minding her post
at the Library of Congress, who
shrugged off the question of what we'd be
reading at century's end: "By the year 2000
nobody will be reading poems." Thus she
prophesied. End of that
interview! End of the world
as we know it. Yet, how can I fault
her despair, doing time as she was
in a crumbling Capitol, sirens
and gunfire the nights long, the Pentagon's
stockpile of weapons stacked higher
and higher? No wonder the books
stacked around her began to seem relics.
No wonder she dreamed her own bones
dug up years later, tagged in a museum somewhere
in the Midwest: American Poet—Extinct Species.

Up here in the mountains
we know what extinct means. We've seen
how our breath on a bitter night
fades like a ghost from the window glass.

We know the wolf's gone.
The panther. We've heard the old stories
run down, stutter out
into silence. Who knows where we're heading?
All roads seem to lead
to Millennium, dark roads with drop-offs
we can't plumb. It's time to be brought up short
now with the tale-teller's *Listen:* There once lived
a woman named Delphia
who walked through these hills teaching children
to read. She was known as a quilter
whose hand never wearied, a mother
who raised up two daughters to pass on
her words like a strong chain of stitches.
Imagine her sitting among us,
her quick thimble moving along these lines
as if to hear every word striking true
as the stab of her needle through calico.
While prophets discourse about endings,
don't you think she'd tell us the world as we know it
keeps calling us back to beginnings?
This labor to make our words matter
is what any good quilter teaches.
A stitch in time, let's say.
A blind stitch
that clings to the edges
of what's left, the ripped
scraps and remnants, whatever
won't stop taking shape even though the whole
crazy quilt's falling to pieces.

Fred Chappell

HUMILITY

In the necessary field among the round
Warm stones we bend to our gleaning.
The brown earth gives in to our hands, and straw
By straw burns red aslant the vesper light.

The village behind the graveyard tolls softly, begins
To glow with new-laid fires. The children
Quiet their shouting, and the martins slide
Above the cows at the warped pasture gate.

They set the tinware out on checkered oilcloth
And the thick-mouthed tumblers on the right-hand side.
The youngest boy whistles the collie to his dish
And lifts down the dented milk pail:

This is the country we return to when
For a moment we forget ourselves,
When we watch the sleeping kitten quiver
After long play, or rain comes down warm.

Here we might choose to live always, here where
Ugly rumors of ourselves do not reach,
Where in the whisper-light of the kerosene lamp
The deep Bible lies open like a turned-down bed.

FOREVER MOUNTAIN

J. T. Chappell, 1912–1978

Now a lofty smoke has cleansed my vision.

I see my father has gone to climb
Easily the Pisgah slope, taking the time

He's got a world of, making spry headway
In the fresh green mornings, stretching out
Noontimes in the groves of beech and oak.
He has cut a walking stick of second-growth hickory
And through the amber afternoon he measures
Its shadow and his own shadow on a sunny rock.
  Not marking the hour, but observing
The quality of light come over him.
He is alone, except what voices out of time
Come to his head like bees to the bee-tree crown,
The voices of former life as indistinct as heat.

By the clear trout pool he builds his fire at twilight,
And in the night a granary of stars
Rises in the water and spreads from edge to edge.
He sleeps, to dream the tossing dream
Of the horses of pine trees, their shoulders
Twisting like silk ribbon in the breeze.

He rises glad and early and goes his way,
Taking by plateaus the mountain that possesses him.

My vision blurs blue with distance,
I see no more.
Forever Mountain has become a cloud
That light turns gold, that wind dislimns.

  This is a prayer.

NARCISSUS AND ECHO

Shall the water not remember *Ember*
my hand's slow gesture, tracing above *of*
its mirror my half-imaginary *airy*
portrait? My only belonging *longing;*
is my beauty, which I take *ache*

away and then return, as love   *of*
teasing playfully the one being   *unbeing.*
whose gratitude I treasure   *Is your*
moves me. I live apart   *heart*
from myself, yet cannot   *not*
live apart. In the water's tone,   *stone?*
that brilliant silence, a flower   *Hour,*
whispers my name with such slight   *light:*
moment, it seems filament of air,   *fare*
the world become cloudswell.   *well.*

THE STORY

Once upon a time the farmer's wife
told it to her children while she scrubbed potatoes.
There were wise ravens in it, and a witch
who flew into such a rage she turned to brass.

The story wandered about the countryside until
adopted by the palace waiting maids
who endowed it with three magic golden rings
and a handsome prince named Felix.

Now it had both strength and style and visited
the household of the jolly merchant
where it was seated by the fire and given
a fat gray goose and a comic chambermaid.

One day alas the story got drunk and fell
in with a crowd of dissolute poets.
They drenched it with moonlight and fever and fed it
words from which it never quite recovered.

Then it was old and haggard and disreputable,
carousing late at night with defrocked scholars
and the swaggering sailors in Rattlebone Alley.
That's where the novelists found it.

SHARKS

> " '. . . [A]ll angel is not'ing more dan de shark
> well goberned.' "
> —Fleece in *Moby-Dick*

You have to keep them under close watch.
They attack without warning, sudden as a squall,
underslung jaws swinging loose on the gilled latch

like a baby getting ready to bawl
its head off. Treading time, they circle the sole
survivor, never doubting he'll fall

from grace soon enough, dizzied by their sunlit shoal.
Light yaws and tacks, blown back against his battered vision
by the wind their fins wake. Whole

days drift by, like seaweed. Though history seems to shun
him, and sunburn raises blisters on his mouth,
he sucks salt from the Pacific Ocean

as a baby pulls a breast. Sharks swim south
of Paradise, around the Cape of Sin,
but he who clings like a barnacle to the lessons of his youth

earns the salute of a scaly fin.
He may yet teach a school of hammerheads
to dance on the head of a pin.

PHYLOGENESIS

She cracks her skin
like a shell, and goes in

She camps in her womb
She sucks the marrow from her bones

and sips bison's blood
in the afternoon; for years,

snow piles outside the cave she burrows in
She wakes to warm weather,

fur on her four feet, grass
rising and falling in waves like water

She feeds on flowering plants,
enjoys a cud of orchid and carrot

In the Middle Permian, scales slippery as shale appear
on her back; her spine unfurls a sail broadside

to the sun, filling with a light like wind, while *Sphenodon*
turns its third eye on the sky, sensing

rain, and rock salt washes into the ocean
Silent as mist, she slides down a mud bank on her underbelly

Lobe-finned and fleshy,
she pumps air through her gills

She's soft as jelly
Her skull is limestone

She drifts, like a continent
or a protozoan, on the planet's surface,

and sinks into the past
like a pebble into a brackish pool

The seas catch fire
The earth splits and gapes

The earth cracks open like an egg
and she goes in

We begin

WORK

The old dog, Work, one eye blind as if seeing
wore it out, a limp in his hindquarters,
lies on his stomach on the floor at your slippered feet,
content merely to dream in your presence.

In his old age, the fur on his paws has grown
so long he, too, seems to have on slippers.
When you reach down to rub his wary ears,
he sends you a secret message of gratitude.

Strange to be here so idly, after the days
of long walks, of chasing squirrels and sticks.
The days of hunting down reluctant quarry.
There were many days when he was your one companion.

It is you who should thank him, and so you do,
inwardly. His eyes as they look up at you
are unspoken words; the blind one surely says
love. He rests his muzzle on his paws.

It may snow tonight. The storm windows
muffle the racket of the semis as they speed
past your house toward Illinois; the fire in
the fireplace makes a warm spot on the dog's coat,

you are warmed by both the fire and your dog
while candles burn and the coffee kettle heats.
It is as if your whole house is on fire
with a fire that does not burn or hurt.

This is home, where you and your old dog, Work,
hang out together, especially in autumn,
when the late tomatoes are killed by frost
and smoke from your chimney spirals into night.

THE REVELATION AT HAND

A century closes—guilty twentieth
Of twenty Yeats described—but nothing returns.
There is nothing that will repeat itself
As a pattern on the pane through which we gaze
These days at dark rain falling on a facing
Of red rock, where rooks caw. Nothing comes back
To be born again. Our horrors are ever new—
Or else, I think, they are the same horrors
They always were, unchanged, continuous.
The rain blackens the brick chimney, like soot,
Or as if blood could burn to ash, and in smoke
And black rain one reads only contamination,
The slow leakage of scientific empires,
A wasting like Chernobyl, an unconcern.

No child now teaches us, to make us parents
Of a new philosophy, or enacts innocence,
That we might recover that drowned country
From the blood-tide. Nor, in desert sands, stirs
There some meaning, amid winged, turning shadows,
Which, though we must fail to comprehend
Its monstrous fullness, reveals anything at all,
Except its lion body, human head.

MY ROMANTIC LEGERDEMAIN

Who are these women, and why do they spread
such vicious truths? I speak only for myself,
and even that may imply too firm a judgment.

Wife after suburban wife tumbles in liquid
disarray, framing the blank release of breath, the desire
to live out each plot, inhabit each house and life,

but lightly. Into this rises love, random and existential,
reliant upon a chance complicity of coordinates
and my own unquiet heart. Karen told me,

one toxic night when I was melancholy,
you must learn to be aloof, don't let them see,
don't let them know your needs

or even that you have them. Ellen said go
find the grownups and play with them; she told me
stories about lives I could have known. Sometimes

I live in a field of stars, novae in bloom, a cascade
of sixteenth notes punching through the clueless
sky, but when I rest, the women inside begin

again, talking about a certain quickness of hand,
about time without nostalgia, numbers greater
than one, a life outside parentheses.

Joshua Clover

THE MAP ROOM

We moved into a house with 6 rooms: the Bedroom,
the Map Room, the Vegas Room, Cities
in the Flood Plains, the West, & the Room Which Contains All
of Mexico. We honeymooned in the Vegas Room where
lounge acts wasted our precious time. Then there was the junta's
high command, sick dogs of the Map Room, heel-
prints everywhere, pushing model armies into the unfurnished
West. At night: stories of their abandoned homes in the Cities
in the Flood Plains, how they had loved each other
mercilessly, in rusting cars, until the drive-in went under.
From the Bedroom we called the decorator & demanded
a figurehead . . . the one true diva to be had
in All of Mexico: Maria Felix [star of *The Devourer,* star
of *The Lady General*]. Nightly in Vegas, "It's Not Unusual"
or the Sex Pistols medley. Nothing ever comes back
from the West, it's a one-way door, a one-shot deal,—
the one room we never slept in together. My wife
wants to rename it The Ugly Truth. I love my wife for her
wonderful, light, creamy, highly reflective skin;
if there's an illumination from the submerged Cities,
that's her. She suspects me of certain acts involving Maria Felix,
the gambling debts mount . . . but when she sends the junta off to Bed
we rendezvous in the Map Room & sprawl across the New World
with our heads to the West. I sing her romantic melodies from the Room
Which Contains All of Mexico, tunes which keep arriving
like heaven, in waves of raw data, & though I wrote
none of the songs myself & can't pronounce them, these are my greatest hits

Rosanne Coggeshall

TO JOHN BERRYMAN

I

Two nights the dog has roomed in rain
  Beautiful & red.   Simple grow
The sleeves of this old shirt.
Dust forms windows in the floor.
Henry's book hurt   helped   is more.
Somewhere she is curling into sleep.
Not too rainy   Henry   not too deep.

II

Henry I have finished yr sad songs
& they are   mostly   sad
& songs   to here   around the wrinkle
Of a chord that grows a muscle
& is strong: chords of wrists reck
Blood & buckle into breath
That feathers flutes.
Show me someone sings
I show you bones what float.

But yr bones hit ice.
I wonder which broke first.
The sick grow lame in aim I think:
Sick. But only silver hacksaws tell.
I wall easily. Glass grows emptily
In twos   in threes   but   Henry
There are trees in the window
There are trees.

Nicole Cooley

ROMANCE

On the train to New Orleans my sister and I
light the Virgen de Guadalupe candles
and the line of unlucky women steps out from the flame.

They file past at the window where we sit,
where we have given up being safe from them,
our four aunts with their loose dresses for mourning,

their fasting, their silent refusals. These women loved
their grief like the bread they would not let themselves eat,
like the children they would not allow into their bodies.

We know their unspoken lesson—take nothing
into the body. We know they will wait for us,
a line of dolls cut from the same sheet of butcher paper,

the sisters of this family linked by their hands and alone.
One mile into Mississippi, the train passes a statue
of blue-robed Mary in someone else's yard, bathtubs leaning

against the wire fence. I place us there. With relief,
I lower each of us into the bath, into the crystal salts.
Oil pools on the surface of the water. Sulfur is staining our skin.

The train drags on across the tracks, away from us,
leaving us in our own story. My first aunt looks down
at the flat pan of her pelvis, strung tight between hipbones

she'll never touch. She likes her body empty and clean.
Coaxing her into the tub, we preach the virtues of this water,
its power to wash away sin. The second one taps

her cigarette ash on the grass and blows smoke at the sky
while we plead with her about drowning,
tell her not to go all the way down. Why should she listen?

We know how good the body can feel, unused, expecting
nothing. But my sister and I are trying to prove them wrong.
When I kneel beside my family, I am desperate.

My sister drags the sign of the cross in the dirt
with a stick. Why don't we quit telling the story?
Once upon a time there were four princesses and a single

safe tower. No prince. In place of a man, a basket
of primroses they ripped into pieces, four finches
fighting it out for the kingdom. In another story,

my sister and I take them all home to New Orleans.
I take them all into me, my secret collection.
I give up. They live in my body. Oh, we are beautiful.

In the real story, we are all starving together. Sisters,
the wafer floats on my tongue like bad luck, like our name.

John William Corrington

ON MY 18TH BIRTHDAY

this is the sum of it:

> what i can expect
> from bones has
> succinctly arrived

skin has done its

> part

time of gratuities is ending:
>   tony's sister will ask
>   for a fin; free juice is
>   memory; a lump of boy
>   is snuffling in my
>   throat

birthday

>   ends a barefoot deluge
>   of
>   interminable dry runs:
>   the next rap could be scary and adult; the
>   next misstep may draw
>   some of my wonderful
>   blood

my analyst
>   a black barber who sips
>   adrenalin
>   and barbecues like a god

> gave me a slip of paper
> tied with some dental
> floss:

>   for birthday

it said
    —you must have learned
        you can eat almost anything
            and almost everything
            will certainly try to
        eat you
            this is for the winner
            to clean his teeth

from now on a haircut is six bits

Stephen Cushman

BLUE PAJAMAS

I perform the offices of comfort
as best I can. My wife away,
he moans through the corridor
at four in the morning, *Lie down with me,*
I'm lonely. In this matter, I know I am
his second choice, my face a face
no razor makes a mother's, my breath
always a father's breath.
Still, I lie down with the lamb
he sleeps with again, now that he knows
a second baby's coming, and wait
for the short, shallow intakes of air
to deepen their draw
through the well of his belly.

I put it all on the line
one piece at a time. The sun not up,
wet laundry stings my hands, stiffening
the fingers that squeeze open clothespins
as though I'd suffered a stroke. *Will you die?*
he asks over breakfast. *If you and Mommy die,*
I'll be lonely. In the wind
his sleepsuit flicks its members
faster than in tantrums, fluttering
jay-blue cotton against the Judas trees
that lathered pink last week. At bedtime
the cotton smells purged of his body
folded on my lap. *Lie down with me,*
he whispers. In the dark
after the book
I kiss my final kiss.

FUNK

Opening the diaper, each morning
becomes the third day, when God
created the earth, late
in the afternoon, mountains
and continents firmly in place,
the waterways swinging between,
He turned His attention
to the lowlands, malodorous
and steamy, the swampy
muck of undersides mutating
already into something new,
future home of the uncivilized
creatures who will sleep in their own
dung and arise unfazed, a dazzling
smile ripping through the bars
of the crib, sunlight breaking
like tears on their slithering
bodies and their unhaired heads.

THE MASTER PRINTER

Though it's May it is the first spring day.
You are giving me a crossbar to school.
I am wondering will Adolina Davy or Lily Walsh
notice me in my first long pants.
We weave through fuming, hooting cars,
elated we've outwitted lunchtime traffic.
Our new front wheel is answering the sun.

You inquire am I okay as I wriggle.
I confide it's just my behind is a bit sore.
You laugh & say we haven't far to go.
But I never want to get there.
We wave each other off & I run pell-mell
to buy a pennyworth of Bull's Eyes,
escaping the thought of the line-up bell.

I hide the sweets beneath my inkwell,
but my nothing-to-hide look reveals them
to the all-seeing eyes of Brother Dermot.
He smiles, ordering me to put out one hand
& then the other, caning
until both palms are stinging pulps,
as he has beaten so many, so often,

distorting each palm's destiny.
Did that brother harm you too
by continually summoning you in
to declare that I, your son, was a *bit* slow?
He did not know, blind behind a frown,
that you had the master printer's skill
of being able to read backwards & upside down.

Alison Hawthorne Deming

SCIENCE

Then it was the future, though what's arrived
isn't what we had in mind, all chrome and
cybernetics, when we set up exhibits
in the cafeteria for the judges
to review what we'd made of our hypotheses.

The class skeptic (he later refused to sign
anyone's yearbook, calling it a sentimental
degradation of language) chloroformed mice,
weighing the bodies before and after
to catch the weight of the soul,

wanting to prove the invisible
real as a bagful of nails. A girl
who knew it all made cookies from euglena,
a one-celled compromise between animal and plant,
she had cultured in a flask.

We're smart enough, she concluded,
to survive our mistakes, showing photos of farmland,
poisoned, gouged, eroded. No one believed
he really had built it when a kid no one knew
showed up with an atom smasher, confirming that

the tiniest particles could be changed
into something even harder to break.
And one whose mother had cancer (hard to admit now,
it was me) distilled the tar of cigarettes
to paint it on the backs of shaven mice.

She wanted to know what it took,
a little vial of sure malignancy,

to prove a daily intake smaller
than a single aspirin could finish
something as large as a life. I thought of this

because, today, the dusky seaside sparrow
became extinct. It may never be as famous
as the pterodactyl or the dodo,
but the last one died today, a resident
of Walt Disney World where now its tissue samples

lie frozen, in case someday we learn to clone
one from a few cells. Like those instant dinosaurs
that come in a gelatin capsule—just add water
and they inflate. One other thing this
brings to mind. The euglena girl won first prize

both for science and, I think, in retrospect, for hope.

NO. 18

from *The Monarchs: A Poem Sequence*

In Mexico where the eastern monarchs
gather for their winter sleep,
a tide of fluttering orange and black
sweeping over the border and into the trees
of the central mountains, there is
such hunger that the campesinos,
though their fathers and mothers
believe the butterflies are
spirits of the dead returning,
must cut the forest for fuel and cropland.
Brush smoking, burned pits of stumps,
scrawny pony, burro tethered in the cut corn.
So much of the sanctuary has been lost

that experts have begun to issue
the usual decrees—how many years to go
before centuries of habit genetically
sealed in butterfly cells will be gone.
In the lofty remains of the cloud forest,
vigilantes guide the pilgrims under the dark canopy
of ancient trees and into the wind of butterfly wings.
In the heat of the afternoon
monarchs come down from their sleep
to huddle on the edges of streams and
meadow pools, trembling to stay warm,
and they sip, then sit, then fly off
until the air is a blizzard of orange.
The pilgrims watch quietly, lines of
schoolchildren from Mexico City,
scientists from Texas and California,
old women in rebozos leaning on the arms
of adult sons, tourists lugging
cameras and binoculars. And together
the visitors drink in the spectacle
with the great thirst they have brought
from their cities and towns, and it is
a kind of prayer, this meeting of our kind,
so uncertain about how to be
the creature we are, and theirs,
so clear in their direction.

R. H. W. Dillard

SHE

(After the English of Jorge Luis Borges)

> In town or field, or by the insatiate sea,
> Men brood on buried loves, and unforgot. . . .
> —H. Rider Haggard

You want her.
You have little to offer:

Your hour under the moon,
The blue asphalt like steel,
The memory you hold of a smile,
Caught like silver in your eye,
A touch of fingers, her hand
Held out from the window
As she leaves (the last time).

A past: dead men, ghosts,
An odor of verbena, "dying thunder of hooves,"
The charge of three hundred men in Peru,
Your father's father wrapped in the hide of a cow,
A soldier shot at Gettysburg,
Caught among boulders, his leg stiff as leather,
The knife his son fashioned,
Touched now with rust, sharp as an eye.

The expression of your books,
The books themselves, green, orange, gold,
The paper stiff as a knee.

Your loyalty
And the fact of your betrayals.

Yourself, the smile no mirror shows,
Safe from time, from joy, from pain.

A glimpse of a yellow rose
In a goblet by a bed.

Your theories of her:
News that opens like a knife, a window,
Authentic and surprising news.

The loneliness that wakes you late and lonely,
The hunger that wakes you,
The lure of uncertainty, danger,
The possibility of defeat.

FOG AT THE SPA

Not the kittenish one you know
From the famous poem

Or the yellow fog
That darkened Eliot's heart

Or the coal-fired fogs
Of the books of our youth

Just this gray mist
That wisps through the balustrade

Floats the distant lake
Into the drifting sky

From the Norwegian *fogge*
Long grass on damp ground

Its blades brush Monique's shoulders
Bare under Maurice's jacket

She shivers as she feels herself
Sinking the tower with its clock

Sinking the steaming mineral springs
Sinking into the moist earth

Where everything is fog
And they are lost and crying

And Maurice's hand is like an iceberg
Calving its fingers slipping away

Like details on a day
When fog fills the long verandas

And memory wraps each minute
In a mist of blurred vision

And Monique is a shadow
And Maurice is a shadow

And the mirror through the window
Mirrors only fog and shadow

Wayne Dodd

LOOKING, LATE AT NIGHT

Like some bleached photograph
at the bottom of an old box labeled "Women's
Underwear: Pink Step-ins." It is all
so indistinct, so
grainy: a frame house, possibly
white, low weeds running away
from the hollyhocks bordering the surrounding
porch. Dust, glare, heat—nothing else
anywhere: no other houses, no trees, no
one dying of cancer in some airless room
out of sight.
Perhaps also the sound
of horses, snorting their sharp rejection
of our airs. It is a farm,
surely, but where
are the people,
the small women in unseen
step-ins, the gaunt men
in black suits rusted
with dust? In the barn?
In the bedroom? In some other
picture?
But this is
the picture, this the one
scene that keeps on rising
at night, like a summons,
calling me out into the white spaces beyond
this narrow focus,
to where I imagine I will find my
self, lying darkly among the pale weeds
and sunflowers, like some deep-red psyche
of the tropics, just dying
to blossom.

EASY

While she starts the water and measures the pasta,
he sets the table and peels the garlic.
She cuts up broccoli, strips snow peas, readies fish—
he presses the garlic, fixes her a kir, and him a gin.
She sautés the vegetables while he grates cheese,
readies the candles, and puts flowers on the table.
She puts pasta in the boiling water, and fixes salad,
which he takes to the table with the cheese.
She mixes a salad dressing, he opens the wine
and takes it to the table, where everything is ready,
except for the pasta, so he lights the candles
and puts salad from a big walnut bowl into small ones.

Now she or he brings the pasta, greens and fish
mixed in, and they sit to talk, drink wine and eat.
Though October, they sit on a small screen porch
in the back of the house where they have lived
for twelve years of their twenty together,
the last six, the children gone, alone.
Once, during dinner, if they stop talking
and listen to the music, they may, without drama,
hold hands a moment, almost like a handshake
by now, most friendly, confirming the contract,
and more. She is a pretty woman of 51, who has
kept herself trim and fit. He is 56 and hasn't.

Later, they will clear the dishes and clean up,
and she will bring tea and fresh fruit to bed,
where they will watch a little television or not,
with herbal tea and the fruit. After that, if
they make love or not, they will talk a long time,
her work or his, the budget, the Middle East,
this child or that, how good dinner was, how
easy it is, the times like this, when it's simple.

Wallace Fowlie

MARCEL IN VENICE

It was in Venice where my grief was cured,
where Albertine no longer lived within
my mind. I ceased to think—those thoughts that once
had tortured me—of what she might have done
with other girls, and then those kisses she
had once bestowed upon my throat grew dim
and faded from my memory.

                I watched
a rose-cheeked girl who sold Venetian glass
and offered us a range of orange tones.
I long to see her every day, and thought
of bringing her to Paris where I'd keep
her jailed for me, and far away from her
piazza flanked by stalwart palaces.

Brendan Galvin

FOR A DAUGHTER GONE AWAY

Today there've been moments
the earth falters and almost
goes off in those trails of smoke
that resolve to flocks so far
and small they elude my naming.
Walking the old Boston & Maine
roadbed, September, I understand
why it takes fourteen
cormorants to hold the bay's
rocks down. Have I told you
anything you ought to know?
In time you'll come to learn
that all clichés are true, that
a son's a son till he marries,
and a daughter's a daughter
all her life, but today
I want to begin Latin 1 with you
again, or the multiplication
tables. For that first phrase of
unwavering soprano that came
once from your room, I'd suffer
a year of heavy metal. Let all
who believe they're ready for
today call this sentimentality,
but I want the indelible
print of a small hand
on the knees of my chinos again,
now that my head's full of
these cinders and clinkers
that refused fire's refinements.
I wish I could split myself
to deepen and hold on as

these crossties have, and admit
goatsbeard and chicory,
bluecurls and blazing star,
those weeds of your never quite
coming back. I wish I could stop
whatever's driving those flocks
and drove the B & M freights into air.

POCOCURANTE

Word for the ringsnake
I found in a burl
just under the woodpile tarp,
folded like a black mat of
witches' butter fungus,
trying to shunt itself
its own failing heat, asleep,
so I worked around it,
splitting the pile and facing
the open sides up elsewhere
until, a foot long, longer,
snake poured itself through
itself, down one layer, showing
a yellow collar, and curled
again between two rounds,
buried its head, pococurante,
caring little, like a
stove-settled dog, and as its
tenements disappeared
with the afternoon, spilled
down oak, layer by layer, all
the way to damp earth,
where, discombobulous, it rolled
and stiffened, yellow belly
up, one of those gimp

lanyards woven in childhood,
and I made it a teepee of
bark sleeves to withdraw
from October in, and went away.

THE GANDY DANCERS

Not men but *guys,* we knew it even then,
four of them, unshaven and eating sandwiches,
giving the thermos jugs a workout. Coming back
from the pond sometimes, we'd find them where
the sand road crossed the Boston & Maine rails,
lounging by a yellow machine that looked like
a movie catapult with a pirate ship's bilge pump
thrown in just in case. Always with time for kids,
they'd promise "a ride when you're old enough,"
and climb aboard. Two working the seesaw
of the handles, shirttails flapping, they'd pump
out into the heat until it melted them to mirage,
and on through scrublands where only the deer
saw them, and among the little blue-eyed lakes
and cranberry bogs, out over bridges where
rivers ran beneath the ties, everywhere a kid
wanted to go, *coureurs de bois,* as in our stories.
As if anybody ever wanted to be a cop or lawyer
before Detroit and Dallas got together
and jimmied up the miles of blue glinting steel,
leaving unhealed roadbed, leaving a morning when
you wouldn't wake up wondering where
those guys were, and couldn't imagine the striped arm
dropping in front of traffic anymore, the synchronized
red flashers and dinging, and you on your yellow
machine, waving to the kid behind his father's
windshield waving, crouched by your black tin lunchbox,
all you'd ever need to ramble through this life.

TOAD

Trencherman of the moist places,
I never find you at home in your cracked
flowerpot under the day lilies,
but drinking through your skin, asleep
or unperturbed by my shoe in a wet furrow.
To live you have to bury yourself
alive sometimes, risking a tine when
I fork the compost and the earth
caves there and quakes. Undercover cop
of the garden, you are serious
as a samurai, and shoot from the lip,
cleaning up on ten thousand pests
in a good season. Have a couple of
spittlebugs, chase them down
with a red-banded leaf-hopper or two,
but lay off those geishas the ladybugs,
who have work of their own to do.
Were you dropped here, a meteorite
of green-crusted ore? Nights
when the moon's your color, I imagine
Japan, and a farmer who throws
the first cup from the bottle
into his fields as a welcome to you.

George Garrett

MAIN CURRENTS OF AMERICAN POLITICAL THOUGHT

Gone then the chipped demitasse cups
at dawn, rich with fresh cream and coffee,
a fire on the hearth, winter and summer,
a silk dandy's bathrobe, the black Havana cigar.

Gone the pet turkey gobbler, the dogs and geese,
a yard full of chickens feeling the shadow of a hawk,
the tall barn with cows and a plough horse, with corn,
with hay spilling out of the loft, festooning the dead Pierce Arrow.

Gone the chipped oak sideboards and table,
heavy with plenty of dented, dusty silverware.
Gone the service pistol and the elephant rifle
and the great bland moosehead on the wall.

"Two things," you told me once, "will keep
the democratic spirit of this country alive—
the free public schools and the petit jury."
Both of these things are going, too, now, Grandfather.

You had five sons and three daughters,
and they are all dead or dying slow and sure.
Even the grandchildren are riddled with casualties.
You would not believe these bitter, shiny times.

What became of all our energy and swagger?
At ninety you went out and campaigned for Adlai Stevenson
in South Carolina. And at my age I have to force
myself to vote, choosing among scoundrels.

SNAPSHOT: ITALIAN LESSON

When I hear of the death of a major poet these days,
I remember Rome, 1958, myself standing alongside an enormous priest
by a newspaper kiosk in Trastevere, staring at headlines—
IL PAPA E MORTO! As the priest turns away a voice from the crowd
(all too poor to buy a paper) calls out: "Is it true the Holy Father is dead?"
The priest nods, then shrugs hugely and answers in the local dialect:
"Better him than us, eh? Better him than us." And walks off to his chores
among the poor who are always with us even until the end of the world.

THE DRUM MAJORETTE MARRIES
AT CALVARY BAPTIST

She goes blind down the aisle.
Candles prick the twilight
banks of gladioli, fern, and baby's breath.
Abloom in polyester peau de soie,
she smiles a starlet smile, clings
to her wet-eyed daddy's beef.
The organ metes her steps in groans.
Her mother wrings a tissue in her lap.
The groom, monolith to the white cloud
she is, waits at the altar. His Adam's
apple bobs. He is a straight, black
prop incidental to this script.

Outside, night falls over the tableau
the flashbulbs freeze as the couple
ducks through showers of seed
and runs for the idling limousine.
Before the door clicks shut on all her gauze,
in the strange light the white dress
seems to drift like petals piece by piece,
until out of the net the drum majorette
pumps her knees. Her trim boots dart,
her white gloves slice
at cacophonies of dark.
Her silver whistle flashes, shrills.

SPARROW

In the town streets
pieces of the perishing world
Pieces of the world coming into being

The peculiar angle at which a failing gutter descends
from a house-eave; a squirrel's surviving tattered nest of leaves
woven into a high bare crook of an elm tree
      (the last one alive on this street);

the small bright green leafing out of that elm;
a man shaking coins in a dry Coke-cup and saying
Small change, brother? Small change?;
                    a woman
in scuffed white running shoes and a fine suit hurrying
down the street with a baggy briefcase that must have
papers and her purse and her good shoes inside it
Perhaps a small pistol

Gusts rattle the half-closed upstairs window
      in the old office building that's going to be torn down

Skittering across the sidewalk, a scrap of paper
      with someone's handwriting on it, in pencil
A message that will arrive

Things in themselves

A few minutes of seeing
An exalting

Or a few minutes of complete shelter
A protectedness, a brief rest from the changes

Sparrow moments

~

But this emblem I take from the world—
able, fussing, competing
at the feeder, waiting on a branch,
sudden in flight, looping and rushing, to another branch,
quick to fight over mating and quick at mating,
surviving winter on dry dead seed-heads of weeds
and around stables and garbage and park benches,
near farms and in deep woods,
brooding in summer-hidden nests—house sparrow,

song sparrow, fox sparrow, swamp sparrow,
field sparrow, lark sparrow, tree sparrow, sage sparrow,
white-throated sparrow of the falling whistled song
that I hear as a small reassurance—

Would my happiness be that the sparrow not be emblem—
that it be in my mind only as it is outside of my mind, itself,
that my mind not remove it from itself
into realms of forms and symbolic thinking?

My happiness, that is, my best being

Words like branches and leaves,
or words like the birds among
the branches and leaves?

They take wing all at once
The way they flee makes flight look like exuberance not fear
They veer away around a house-corner

THE AFFECT OF ELMS

Across the narrow street from the old hotel that now
houses human damage temporarily—
deranged, debilitated, but up and around in their odd
postures, taking their meds, or maybe trading them—

is the little park, once a neighboring mansion's side yard,
where beautiful huge old elm trees, long in that place,
stand in a close group over the mown green lawn
watered and well kept by the city, their shapes expressive:

the affect of elms is of struggle upward and survival,
of strength—despite past grief (the bowed languorous arches)
and torment (limbs in the last stopped attitude of writhing)—

while under them wander the deformed and tentative
persons, accompanied by voices, counting their footsteps,
exhaling the very breath the trees breathe in.

EARTH ELEGY

Rain on the shingles, on the maples—
this evening,
                    ground fog and cloud
mingled in the hollow between the ridges,
and a sorrow so gentle it could be

the mud I took this morning into my hands,
lifting it
                    from the garden's slump
of soil and rind, from its cursive sprawl
of blackened vine, turning the garden

after hard frost seared from purple
to black
                    the last cosmos.
I put down the shovel and took the damp
earth into my hands—

and when I broke the soft clay open
found
                    this twist of root
left out of last year's harvest, sown over
in spring, refired in the kiln of summer.

A hardened crust, nearly hollow. A blind
bounded thing,
                    so singular
nothing might divine it. *This is my body
broken*—once a sentence of breath

spun so vividly round I could put it
on my tongue,
                    and the words would

halo and hallow and blur my descent
into the barrow of unknowing

each moment is. No words now. Only this
root, humped
                      like a burial mound
and the hush of wondering what to pray,
knowing full well I have not loved

I have not suffered, endangered, or enjoyed
enough of this world
                              to relinquish it
for another only made real by dying, or by
living in the holy world of words, apart

from what they point to. Here now, just
beyond the window glass,
                                      evening grosbeaks
gust and go. On the sill of the quiet rain
I put the root, and I sit with it,

into the night watching and waiting,
letting whatever words come
                              go off
on a spool of breath—until, silken
and sudden, from the pith

comes forth, nodding on its stem of dawn,
this day,
            unfolding itself
into the dark like a lily. And I sense
the quick of it, so tenderly nearing

it brushes aside its own icon screen
of bloom and root,
                      black and gold—
and I am, crown to bole, just this sun
so recklessly arising.

GLASS ELEGY

The day she went mad, she watched white sun
emerge from the oaks, shaking loose
the dark as you'd knock garden dirt from an onion.
At breakfast, though we're just now putting in seed,
her talk ran to harvest.

             Out here, she said, *I'm transparent,*
a single bloom in a glass bowl of water. I don't need
mirrors, I don't need field.

Later she came back to the house, scattered.
Her hands had flown from her like birds in high wind,
vanishing in a rent of air between trees.

During the worst she lost her eyes,
her ears, her tongue. The glass bowl cracked. She couldn't
recover her collarbone, her right foot, her left breast.
And because I'd learned to talk to her as I would
to myself alone in a room, I tried
to go with her, eyes shut
into the suck of black wind.

Hold still! she cried.

She'd been so long in front of mirrors,
an image in glass, a glass bloom
in a bowl—

             and when she broke through,
the woods moved in quick, everything out there
verb, quicksilver changes. And these swallow you
unless you turn mirror yourself, and the world
flashes from you each moment.

And then she was quiet.

I can't account for her words that morning, what she later
saw, or the calm finally out of which she spoke
with such authority.

She described a random, long walk in the afternoon
when the woods breathed with her
and she lived through the power
of death and the earth's
rotation

as ordinarily
you do, she said, if you're ready to notice.

In the mirror that evening, dark branches tangled
weaving my face with their fire, and almost
I could reach through and touch the ripening

long sweep of wind toward morning.

AT THE RAVINE

Within the interpreted world of stone
walls and a bougainvillea trained to bloom
into the body and beak of a bird,
exotic plumage kept to hand
and rooted, you have pointed out
the prickets of epiphytic bromeliad
kindled by early sun in the spreading tree
across the ravine—candelabra,
you say, smiling to recall
how your mother, new to the language,
said *candle bras*—and so
the conversation rambles into a thicket
of resemblances, nothing singular
but ourselves, and we hide our light.
We have binoculars and two books
to tell us the words for the birds we may
see across the ravine, the land
on the other side gone baroque

with erosion—red rock in twists
of arabesque, open sky, thin pasture.
Nothing stays, nothing keeps us
steady. A white horse dips its neck—
it's a swan. Swan drawn by a child,
faint cirrus and cumulus,
body a cloud propelled across the surface
of a pond in whose depths, as I remember,
the child has drawn the feet, black
and churning, passion and muscle
translated into act—more
exact an emblem than Rilke could give
for the love a woman
feels for a man she can't have,
going away from her, his body
far horizon, ripples of ridges
and hills receding into rain, and yet
the wick of her still burning. Burning.

Look now, you say, *just there—*
and I find the tree as a flash of gold comes
steadily to flame, ripe red
and mango, preening, its back streaked
black and white: clearly oriole,
immature form, none
other like it in the book, we decide.
I lean over the wall, over
the ravine—*barrancosa,* glad to be
warming my hands, reaching across
to a moment of sun embodied, fleet.
We have, seeing the bird,
seen each other, passionate and detached
at once—the way one can take
what comes, love it fully, and setting
free say, yes: *Icterus sclateri.*
Oriole. Magnificent. Yes.

IN THE MARKET

from *Memories of the Future: The Daybooks of Tina Modotti*
1 July 1941

Today on the street I ate a sugared coffin's
sugared child, and in one swallow Guanajuato's ground,
like a gunshot, opened. I was back in the Panteón
I'd toured with Edward, back with the dead.

I can't think what made us go.
With the taste of coffee still in our mouths,
we'd made love. With the straw pattern of the *petate*
imprinted on our skin, we'd washed in the sun.
Down the steps to the fusty vault, I felt his semen
leave me, wet on my thigh. Why would we have wanted
to see bones? That is, I'd expected bones,
not bodies warped in tight skins, in brown
naked hides. Not the scythe of grins, all flesh
made rind. And not the pod of a fetus with its empty
suck at a leathery breast. Edward said,
the ultimate still life, a monumental theme.
But I heard the baby smack its lips, and I fled.

I found myself in the market, touching onions one
by one. I traced silhouettes of shoots and calla stalks
on air, watched one bud split its caul and the white
spathe open. Cold, I let street life slip over me.
I searched each face, in each heard a dry, deathly
smack of the tongue. But I realized for the first time
power—the power to see a world buried in daylight.
I was a lens—and I saw.
           There rose up for me
that day in Guanajuato's streets the dead and the living—
they breathed through my breath, they rinsed through
my pores their blind needs. They were hands
scrubbing clothes, they gripped shovels

and newspapers, lifted cones of bananas, carried
crossbeams on their backs. They went down in the mine
to a source like their mother—they danced in the dust's
brief abundance. Together they endured.

In the street a man shouted a drunken *vacilada,*
hermetic pain pulled inside out, mystical
and snickering like a mescal worm, laughter
that stabbed at the light. *Los muertos mueren,*
y las sombras pasan—"The dead die, shadows pass."
But the air they breathed, we breathe. Their faces
backlight our own, our lives spring up
from their dreams—light
in the work of these thick city streets.

In the center of town I saw
an old rusted pump the color of ocher,
color of bloodstone, ancient as the channel of the vulva,
menstrual color. Near it an old woman in a black
rebozo stacked tortillas on a cloth, a *brasero's*
charcoals glowed, and the old Ford motor
used for grinding the pueblo's corn chugged along.
There was a smell of oil, smoking meat.
I remember the water's iron taste—I used
two hands to pump it. I drank from a gourd.

I thought of lilies—how they pull water clear through
their green channels. In them was presence,
an ease of future. As for me, watching dark water
splash in the dust, wiping my wet chin on my sleeve,
washing my hands in the earth-colored wet—
I'd have struggle, *la lucha.*

James B. Hall

A CLUTCH OF DREAMS

The forked path in the woods
Dreams of a crossroads,
A perfection in concrete, dividing
This valley into four equal fields;

The shoat at the slaughterhouse door
Remembers a fine white gate
At the barn-end of a meadow
And corn calling with the voice of a man.

Waterlogged, the orange liferaft
Drifts on the wide-eyed Pacific
Then sinks, still dreaming of atolls,
And the new crew roistering ashore.

And I, on this forked path
Of dreams, I see fine white gates
And I ride this orange-raft world
Downward towards coral, where all dreams end.

Cathryn Hankla

SWIMMING NAKED

Atlantic skinny-dipping
in the blue moon's full view,
sturdy Venuses yelp and stutter,
brave glistening foam
and old wives' tales of *Don't.*

Drunks stumble on the rocks
to dark river water, twist ankles
to a halt of shivering cold
and somersault beneath the surface
where night fish let gravity go.

Swim through night thoughts
that take away the breath.
Swim through family history
and the last gasp of bad luck.
Swim up, gulp water from a cup.

Some children arch while stroking,
faces awash with fear of loss.
Some learn to clip noses and seek
the slick pool's depth, sinking like
wishes, while mothers cry, "Come up."

THE TAUTOLOGY OF GOODBYE

You say I tend toward silences;
in these rifts, the world

I inhabit is a visual question,
marked by a balancing line
of light on distant water, a mirror
horizon. We afix binoculars
to what is real in this mirage:
a simple fishing rig, sunlight pouring
a swath of sea. I want your
hand to rest in mine, while I test
the real against the as yet
unknown, the present tense against
its picture: as the boat begins
to drift out of our range of vision,
we struggle to distinguish
the ruffles porpoises raise
from the action of waves.
It reminds me of the way our eyes
will try to meet in rearview
mirrors, of the loss I must suffer
whenever someone points
and I turn, but not in time.
I can feel the tugging
of the past in the way your fingers
almost pull away, then stay
to squeeze, and I know
just what it means
to grasp and then let go.

O. B. Hardison, Jr.

KING OF THE WORLD

I have become what I am.
There is now nothing in me that is not what I am.
All my roads lead to me.
I did not expect this to happen.

If I were an oak tree,
My leaves would be children,
Everything I love would be branches,
My enemies would be caterpillars,
My roots would be fastened deep in red clay.
You might then be, say, a bird. Something shining with impossible colors.
I would hold out my branches for you to roost in.
I would grow leaves to shade you.
I would give you my enemies to eat.
My roots would tremble with your singing.

If I were a building, I would have a baroque facade.
My windows would all be clean.
I would have a fountain—
Maybe *The Rape of Europa*—
And children would drink that water.
My walls would have mosaics, my floors *opus Alexandrinum,*
On my ceiling, the apotheosis of Marie Antoinette.
Your word for me would be house.

If I were the shore, every bay would have flags
To celebrate the powers of the sea.
My sand would be at your feet,
I would keep your seashells—
Tulips, razor clams, drills, olives, wentletraps—
For children on summer days.
At night your tide would cover me.

As we mingled, I would say:
Thank you, mother moon;
Thank you, father sun;
Thank you, thank you, thank you.

Every road meanders away from the center.
They all, in one way or another, go past your door.
Drive your triumphant car down any of them.
I will welcome you when you arrive.

William Harmon

WHEN IT COMES

for Norman Maclean

What does it all come down to when it comes?
How do things end that have the grace to end?
The *Iliad* stops with "Hector the breaker of horses";
The last word of *Lord Jim* is "butterflies."

William Hathaway

THE ICEBALL

Mittens tucked fat in my armpit,
I packed it harder and harder to ice
in bare hands. My outraged blood
blazed rosepetal-pink through the skin
of my palms. This one I meant
to throw with all my might
at Larry Darrah's head when they charged.
Anonymous in the arcing blizzard
of snowballs, this one would speed
deadly true to knock his god damn eye
out of his ugly face. Because Darrah
was a cruel prick, that was my scheme.

This bomb was too beautiful: ball-
bearing round, smoother than a crystal
globe, of heft so perfect my arm *knew*
it could not miss, but could not let it go.
I cached it in a niche of our snowfort
to juggle it home in my bare hands
so red yarn from my mittens would not
fuzz it up. O, it was too good for Darrah!
This iceball transcended craft to hold
its own absolute light—a fierce sparkle
too pure for any enemy I knew.

When I took it from the freezer
on the big scorcher in late July
one side had flattened and rough frost
furred its once-slick curves.
The clear glisten had clouded to milky
dun; it had shrunk and smelled

like stale food. Yes, it was interesting
to see it sweat so fast into a cold
puddle on hot cement, how geometric
crystals clung and clarified
in their final blaze. But in those coils
below my stomach where things turn
really disgusting I felt regret—
a miser's loss clogging the pipes.

Ah, that Larry Darrah. He walked ram-
rod straight, like a coke bottle
filled his poop-chute. He chewed
tobacco just to spit it on my pants
and he washed my face with snow
many times, in front of lots of girls.
Teachers loved him and said he was
likely to be elected president one day.
The day I did not knock his damn eye
out was the first time I let this country
down.

DEAR WORDSWORTH

I liked your poems "Michael," "We Are Seven,"
and "Idiot Boy" very much, even when
the teacher read them aloud and cried
and blew her nose. "Tintern Abbey" is really neat,
though I don't understand it. I did a walk-
athon for March of Dimes once. I hate your poem
"Daffodils." Ha-ha, that's just a joke,
I just don't know better because of television.
Seriously, why did you become such a crusty,
old poo-poo? Professor Borck at the university
says you got tired of not being rich. My
dad says poor people are happy being poor

because God loves everyone—even poets. I
think it would be romantic to have a French
girlfriend and a dopefiend for a best friend.
I can hardly wait until my creepy sister
goes to college and I can have her room.
My best friend is Veralee Broussard and I can
talk about anything with her. I wish you
could tell me what it's like to be dead.
It would feel neat to lie in a cozy coffin
underneath the flowers and know everything.
Really, you rot and go to heaven or hell.
Well, this is almost two hundred words, so
I have to go. Tomorrow we read Amy Lowell.
Mrs. Curtis says she smoked cigars!

Robert Hazel

BLACK LEATHER

in memoriam, James Dean

In the merciless sky of his warbled days and nights
clouds imitate dreams the way light poles totem
electric deaths in the sprinkling neon of jukes
over mail-order orphans in their crazy runs through
the wire wheels of motorcycles and the black leather
of shielded rampage, skyrocketed, pledged
by his last ride from California to Indiana
with his untrue Italian girl's yellow scarf tied
to his crash helmet, going to a dirt track's scrambled race
at a little fair, for a small prize, the cloth screaming
behind him from Pasadena to his new gasoline death
ignited in paper cups among roadside weeds and in lean dust
along the monotonous shoulders of a grim highway of corn
spears, his brain suddenly still with this wild love

ON MILES' TRIBUTE TO DUKE

The whole hell is honey my bees strayed to
Flown are the dark larks of Carolina
    & the wired-puppet starlings of Harlem

John Wayne said God went thataway
I never caught up with those horse's asses
I'm still mired down in Baldwin & Florida
I'm not the American who killed the rooster
    that prayed for rain at 4:00 a.m.
    in Black Town
    where bitten dogs weep at dawn

Let the owl scowl
Count wandering armadillos
Count wild berries & busted bicycles
Count dark children as they wince over hot sand to the honey
　　of a church organ, drums & hungry voices
　　calling to a microfilm Jesus in the brain

Robert Hershon

THE PUBLIC HUG

we're leaving the restaurant
and here is an old friend home from spain
we embrace   my luncheon companions
coworkers with the surnames of elizabethan poets
stand aside   later there are jokes about men
who hug men in public

listen: i hug men
i hug women children cats dogs drunks and uncles
i know the texture of people's hair
how much weight their shoulders can support
i'm a patter and a toucher and a kisser
once i playfully punched a friend in the arm
he turned unexpectedly and i smashed his glasses
those are the chances you take

we worked together for four years
maybe bumped in a doorway once
scattering dust from those fragile wings
now i'm gone and you'll never know
whether my hands are hot or cold
so i'll tell you: hot and getting hotter

WE NEVER ASK THEM QUESTIONS

I.

Nelson Rockefeller sends
electric shocks through her body

and puts roaches in her Coca Cola
He has taken her children to Canada
Kirk Douglas has made her live in 60 hotels
His friends find her with their filthy phone calls
She is a Christian
and once worked for an insurance company
Why do they want to destroy her?

2.

He has a neat moustache
and an expensive trenchcoat
and he marches up and down Fifth Avenue
faster than lunch hours
Attached to a small backpack
is a photograph professionally framed
of himself with both eyes blackened
his face cut his shirt bloody
Underneath it says
Look What My Family Did To Me

3.

The old man explains to the subway floor:
All the time something's happening here
there's something happening there
Who the hell could have known that?
What the hell's going on over there?
All the time I'm over here putting on my pants
they're over there putting on their hats

William Heyen

THE MOWER

No more stars are slashed from the hive
of heaven. The evening settles to stillness.
Today the wind's edges swept
the orchard like scythes. Now she rests.

Now the power mower,
drowsing in fumes of gasoline,
though all day her blades whirled
through windfalls under the apple trees;

though she was the great queen to bees
that rose from burrows in the fruit's flesh
to preen for her, to hear
her droning epithalamion;

neither dreams in her dark shed
nor sings mass for the dead, whose wings
are a scatter of stars on the cut grass.
She mows and rests in mindless monotone.

Conrad Hilberry

THE EXPATRIATES

Here in the sun, the long December days
defy sadness. Courtyards, narrow streets,
walls still warm at evening. And flowers—
geraniums, conchas, the bleeding fuchsias—
each with its own faint smell, incense settling
on the cobblestones. The bent arms
of bougainvillaea are tricked out in crimson
or magenta. In the north, we remember,
our grief had reasons: confinement and cold,
the pipes frozen, new snow so deep you wake,
look out, and sink back into the week-long
loneliness. But here on this high plateau,
the air is thin, the clouds thin, the days
attenuated, beaten like gold until
they stretch unbroken from horizon to
horizon. At long distance we hear our children
speaking about their lives. "Really," we say,
"how are you?" "Oh, thanks, I'm all right," sadness,
a voice travelling two thousand miles over
desert and dry riverbed, thinning down
to a single fiber—as in the garden
the orchids lay their small mouths on the neck
of the evening, as grackles scream into the pruned
trees, as lemon tea steeps in the pot
on the wrought-iron table and we talk
of conveniences and inconveniences.
Far away, a dog howls as though
the enchilada woman splashed his eyes
with hot grease. A taxicab backs up
a one-way street, saving gas. The plastered
walls, the cobblestones still warm us. Boys
kick a soccer ball. A woman carries

a car battery on her head. We see
all this as though we were remembering it,
as though the day had stretched on into March
and we were looking back through months
of transparent air. Above the tower
of San Isidro, a weightless scrap of moon
drifts on the sunset like a shallow boat.

Daniel Hoffman

AN ARMADA OF THIRTY WHALES

(Galleons in sea-pomp) sails
over the emerald ocean.

The ceremonial motion
of their ponderous race is

given dandiacal graces
in the ballet of their geysers.

Eyes deep-set in whalebone vizors
have found a Floridian beach;

they leave their green world to fish.
Like the Pliocene midge, they declare

their element henceforth air.
What land they walk upon

becomes their Holy Land;
when these pilgrims have all found tongue

how their canticles shall be sung!
They nudge the beach with their noses,

eager for hedgerows and roses;
they raise their great snouts from the sea

and exulting gigantically
each trumpets a sousaphone wheeze

and stretches his finfitted knees.
But they who won't swim and can't stand

lie mired in mud and in sand,
And the sea and the wind and the worms

will contest the last will of the Sperms.

THE TWENTIETH CENTURY

A squad of soldiers lies beside a river.
They're in China—see the brimmed gables piled
On the pagoda. The rows of trees are lopped
And the Chinese soldiers have been stopped
In their tracks. Their bodies lie
In bodily postures of the dead.

Arms bound, legs akimbo and askew,
But look how independently their heads
Lie thereabouts, some upright, some of the heads
Tipped on their sides, or standing on their heads.
Mostly, the eyes are open
And their mouths twisted in a sort of smile.

Some seem to be saying or just to have said
Some message in Chinese just as the blade
Nicked the sunlight and the head dropped
Like a sliced cantaloupe to the ground, the cropped
Body twisting from the execution block.
And see, there kneels the executioner

Wiping his scimitar upon a torso's ripped
Sash. At ease, the victors smoke. A gash
Of throats darkens the riverbed. 1900. The Boxer
Rebellion. Everyone there is dead now.
What was it those unbodied mouths were saying?
A million arteries stain the Yellow River.

David Huddle

OOLY POP A COW

for Bess and Molly

My brother Charles
brought home the news
the kids were saying
take a flying leap
and eat me raw
and be bop a lula.

Forty miles he rode
the bus there and back.
The dog and I met him
at the door, panting
for hoke poke, hoke
de waddy waddy hoke poke.

In Cu Chi, Vietnam,
I heard tapes somebody's
sister sent of wild thing,
I think I love you
and hey now, what's that
sound, everybody look what's . . .

Now it's my daughters
bringing home no-duh,
rock out, whatever,
like I totally
paused, and like
I'm like . . .

I'm like Mother, her hands
in biscuit dough,

her ears turning red
from ain' nothin butta,
blue monday, and
tutti fruiti, aw rooty!

INSIDE THE HUMMINGBIRD AVIARY

Thumb-sized birds in gaudy greens
iridescent vermilions, stop
on invisible floating dimes
intricately to pivot and kiss

sugar-water bottles or desert
blossoms. Within easy snatching
distance, a Broad-billed perches,
preens, pisses in a quick squirt,

darts out a tongue half
its body length. Suddenly
suspended at breast level,
a Calliope confronts a man,

marking its possession of that
quadrant of space, the sheer force
of its watch-part heart stopping
the giant, making him laugh.

these wings are the furious
energy of perfect stillness
to make him forget kestrels
and red-masked vultures.

here in this airy cage
he has seen five whole

hummingbirds fit
into the chambers

of his hog-sized heart.
What the man wants now
is to be desert soil
beneath a thorny bush,

the black tongues of hummers
engineering sweetness
from blossoms that once
were his body.

T. R. Hummer

SCRUTINY

After the D & C, she stood waiting for a taxi
In the clinic awning's shade. It was afternoon in her
Comfortable little city, early rush hour. She could hear
Traffic beginning to swarm under a bloodless bisected moon.
She was watching everything with singular attention,
Men in their wrinkled suits and skin eclipsed by sweat,
The iridescent black of grackles in the gutter, the bright
Chrome and yellow of a '50s Lincoln at the stoplight,
The ambiguous look on the face of God, the shape of her own hands.
And people looked back at her, she thought, with more
Than casual regard, neither sentimental or curious,
But as if they had something disembodied
In common with her. Suddenly she understood how acts
Of attention corrode the world so the flesh feels scraped away,
Worn thin by the action of light, by the eye.
Suddenly she desired another life, a parallel dimension,
Translucent like our own, but in which the dial of consciousness
Is rotated one counterclockwise click, so every mind possesses
The body immediately to the left. At the corner of Second Avenue
And Royal Street, she paid the driver. He watched her as she vanished
Up the steps of the brownstone, a dominion he will never enter,
An allegory whose other side is blankness.

MY FUNNY VALENTINE IN SPANISH

In the 7–11 parking lot, white boys are terrorized
By a Lincoln stereo punching out 98-decibel jazz. The scene
Reminds them unconsciously of high-art cinema shot
In ferocious blue illumination: the deep wax-job

Of the Continental telegraphing the luster of the streetlights,
The stone-colored lawyer in an elegant linen jacket
Leaning on the fender while the digital self-service pump
Carries on its decisive artifice. Turned up this loud
Past midnight, Miles Davis is a cool apocalypse
Like nothing these boys on stolen skateboards ever entered,
A neighborhood in which no one remembers the depth
Of the æther where antifreeze and motor oil pool,
Or the white ghosts of congressmen obliterating angels' hairs
With their otherworldly logic. This is the music they play
In the tunnels of the underground where subways run
From Cambodia to East L.A. In the barrios, children speak
The subjunctive—*If this were bread, could one eat it?*—
And the love of God is a drug, like the love of death.
The *abuela* behind the 7-11 counter shuffles
And lays out the cards. Her *abuela* taught her this.
Five of clubs, three of diamonds: Every low card
Whispers its password and its alibi. There's an occult
Future here. Somebody makes it. Somebody loves somebody
And crosses the great water for a promise, on a dare.
Rodgers & Hart. The boys on their skateboards listen
To the trumpet whose language nobody taught them.
Mi enamorada graciosa, it might be singing. *Mi corazón.*
One morning somebody wants to blast somebody's lights
Into a pure cobalt vapor floating at the Pleiades' heart,
One morning the cash register and the Lotto machine are eclipsed
By a mist of tear gas–shadowed perfume, the exhaust of the LAPD.
And one morning—Neruda made it past tense in invincible Spanish
That could not translate Franco into hell, or contradict
The bullets that distorted Lorca—*Everything is aflame,
One morning the fires / Come out of the earth / Devouring people.*

    —for Philip Levine

Pinkie Gordon Lane

LYRIC: I AM LOOKING AT MUSIC

It is the color of light,
the shape of sound
high in the evergreens.

It lies suspended in hills,
a blue line in a red
sky.

I am looking at sound.
I am hearing the brightness
of high bluffs and almond
trees. I am
tasting the wilderness of lakes,
rivers, and streams
caught in an angle
of song.

I am remembering water
that glows in the dawn,
and motion tumbled
in earth, life hidden in mounds.

I am dancing a bright
beam of light.

I am remembering love.

Richmond Lattimore

FORLORN DREAM SONG

For John Berryman

This cat never knew
that one, won't never no how now.
But why people go stand on a bridge, teeter
& jump? Whoo,
no way to live. Oh never now
unless somewhere somehow

on a bridge of cloud Peter
slosh us out martinis now for two.
And Henry had it made.
How ever you dream up that metre?
Dropped like a Virgin into your lap? You
got it said.

Meditated on what & went & did it.
Oh we got poets yes we got em still.
There 6s all 4s.
Waiting in line we stand & fidget
for heaven or hell.
Nemmine us, Mr. Bones. No. You got yours.

TUSCARORA 3

Nine years after my mother died,
I went back to where I was,
not when she died, but when
she was dying. At 5 am,
Dennis comes into the house,
stomping his boots. For
the next hour, the sun slits
open the canyon, shines
across 8 cracked miles.

Everybody's mother dies,
that's not what makes me
special. We gave her
a shot at about 2 am.
A spastic crow flew
across the room,
we had to drag her
twitching body back to bed,
clean the trail of shit
she'd splattered in her flight.

Wait. I'm getting ahead
of my story, which isn't
really a story. Everybody's
mother dies; everybody
loves a twisty, turny,
forky road and winds up
looking over their shoulder
at a clean, flat line
between A and B, like
the one that stitches

us to Elko,
through 52 miles of wrinkled hills,
like the folds
of a Weimaraner sleeping
on its side.

Once I gave a poetry reading
with a folk singer. He'd
get the whole room rocking,
rolling, clapping along,
tapping their feet.
Then I'd kick in with a poem
and you've never heard
such silence.
Don't you
have any happy poems?
he wondered. Don't
you know any cancer songs?
I asked.

You have to have
a certain mind to live
in the desert. My mother
didn't care for it. She liked mountains,
lakes, Switzerland. Trees with fruit,
cute shops. When they were plugging
the radium into her mouth,
I was swimming in the mineral quarry.
Ken and I were one year
from getting married,
ten years from divorce,
that old ghost town.

Susan Ludvigson

ON LEARNING THAT CERTAIN PEAT BOGS CONTAIN PERFECTLY PRESERVED BODIES

Under this town's ashes
lies a man, still sweating
the long summer days,
his body
perfect as morning,
even to the bacon and eggs
in his belly.
His skin is damp
in the humid earth,
closed eyes heavier
under rain.
The heart quit pumping early,
but when a rock eases down
and cuts an arm
or grazes his back,
blood still seeps
from the veins,
the clots blooming
like poppies around him.
In the brain
memories lie opened,
one into the other:
the crunch of the ax
as he swings down hard,
his wife calling him in,
a woman singing his name
in the distance.
He does not hear them,
but they are there,

claiming their portions.
By now the wife may be
dead too, the ax passed down
to his son, or rusted
under the woodpile.
The woman cannot recall
her own clear voice
or the features of the man
who should be bones.

POINT OF DISAPPEARANCE

A young man threatens to throw himself
in front of the metro. Weaving, waving
his drunken arms in apparent rage, he yells

at the nearby *clochard,* "I don't want to be saved!"
Meanwhile, onlookers line the quai
in cautious, curious silence. A man, braver

than the rest of us, pulls him back. The boy stays
out of danger long enough to let the train come in
but is pushing the good Samaritan away

when I get on. I watch him lurching, thin
with too-quick growth and all the wrong foods,
I imagine. And I think of that age trimmed

of its myths. At times in a foolish mood
I've said I'd give up all I've learned to be 18 or 19
in Paris, forgetting then how the blood flew

through me like the runaway train I'd seen
in a film, and how the crash was always
a moment away. How the sweet machine

of the body, in perfect ease, could go days
without sleep, but the spirit darkened
quick as a full eclipse before any maze

of choices. A word could sharpen
pain to nearly unbearable grief; a smile
that felt indifferent from one who happened

into my path of attraction was a trial
I might fail, and break down in public, weeping.
Death was an alternative to everyone else's mild

acceptance of the world's devouring
loneliness. Not a few of us considered it.
But now, I read, even more of the young are leaping

from bridges, lying on tracks, their gift
to themselves mere absence
of all that emotion. I see my son lift

his head to examine his awkward presence
in a hall of mirrors. He locates
on a shimmering surface his point of disappearance.

PARIS AUBADE

Breathing, the last possession
that counts, comes faster here, where
time and our oldest obsessions

make us more conscious—self-conscious. The air
is completely polluted, of course, but haze
that descends on this city is like the fair

skin of Doris Day, filmed in the days
when soft light meant dropping gauze
in front of the camera. It's like that these lazy

first weeks when we stay in bed until noon, lawless
as coupling cats we hear on the balcony, late.
We inhale each morning as if the flawed

fabric of earlier lives had been laid
in a drawer, carefully folded, forever.
Yet under the net of that dream, we pay

for what we know. Bodies that flail under covers
all hours in pleasure learn to count breaths—
just after. Though the world falls away for lovers

as they make the escape into flesh,
its heavy atmosphere fills them. Clouds
are the color of nipples. Worn silk thins to mesh.

LASTING

When the first radio wave music escaped Earth's ionosphere, it literally did become
eternal. Music, in this century, has been converted from sound into the clarity of
pure light. Radio has superseded the constraints of space.
—Leonard Shlain, *Art & Physics*

Imagine Vivaldi suddenly falling
on the ears of a woman
somewhere beyond Alpha Centauri,
her planet spun into luminescence
aeons from now. She might be
much like us, meditating
on the body, her lover murmuring
to the underside of her breast
before its heaviness suspends,
for a moment, the lift and pause
of his breath. A music she almost knows
drifts through centuries, startling,

augmenting her pleasure.
When earth is particles of dust,
Orson Welles may still strike fear
into the hearts of millions
who wake one morning, unaware
that light has arrived
as an audible prank. Ezra Pound might rasp
his particular madness from an Italy
still alive in arias that shower
into the open windows
of a world youthful as hope.
When books are no longer even ashes,
and no heart beats in any space
near where we were, suns
may intersect, and some of our voices
blend into choirs, the music of the spheres
adrift among new stars.

Martha McFerren

TELL ME

Meet a stranger by night
and he'll ask a riddle.
Why should he want to know
what's deeper than the sea?
Why does that troll ask
what's whiter than milk
when he could munch you
under the bridge
without philosophizing?
Stretch the metaphor,
says the bearded devil,
or else, pretty lady,
you're not god's—
you're one of mine.
But he, too, is metaphor.

To save yourself
keep them jabbering till dawn.
Match their riddles
to the infinite power
until they freeze in sunlight
or drop to befuddled ash.
Vocabulary's the answer.
Rise on specifics, pretty lady,
since language is god's earth
and god the better word.

Tell me: will you rise
till there's no metaphor,
no question, no god at all,
only a full definition?

Will you rise till there's
no false knight on the road,
only yourself
grown sharper than a thorn?

David Middleton

THE FAMILY TREE

for my "country grandmother," d. 1962

It always brought the fall to you off guard,
This old pecan, its brown husks clustered hard,
While on the lawn's high grass leaves crisp and bent
Touched nuts and newborn moths with bitter scent.
More quickly then, as if you'd been delayed,
You'd gather cabbage in the evening shade
And dig up late potatoes with your spade
In a garden that you planted near the end
From pride and need. Just there is where I sinned,
Though still a city boy who could not read
The seasons' book of hours and took no heed,
For once in bright July, in my Sunday suit
I climbed the pecan and plucked unready fruit
Smushing the pulp inside each pliant hull,
Eating rubbery nuts until so sick and full
I ran to you as you read your Bible verses
On the long front porch, your innocent curses
Holding me as you turned to where time weaves
Births and deaths and weddings in the leaves.
Then, distracting me from a stomach so torn
You traced the family tree till I was born
Once more. "Don't pick too soon" was all you said
As distant winds blew faintly overhead,
Yet only now, so far from summer calm,
The hard brown hulls held tight in my hard palm,
Can I suspect how soon you saw the end
To which all family trees and world-trees tend
In an old pecan, which, when the fall winds cry,
Shreds its dead cocoons against the sky.

BLUE HERONS

for Carolyn

The morning sun inclines us toward its light
Spreading above scrub willow and the sedge
Where swamp gives way at last to marshy ponds
Of pickerel, fire flag, and arrowhead.
And there in mangle-brush and roseau cane,
Black mangrove, matted bullrush, and the dense
Old water-groves of tupelo and gum
Or high within the doming cypress-stands
We see the great blue herons in their nests,
Each platform with its clutch of pale green eggs.

Hatched out in June with softest natal down,
The birds become tall stalkers in their prime
Deliberate in movement through the pools
Darting at minnows, frogs, and dragonflies.
Their colonies remain throughout the year
Though when their northern kin who breed in cold
Then gaze toward polar wastes of ice and snow
Are drawn back south by some still hidden sign
Our residents call out while they return
Alighting on the islands and the coast.

We make no noise yet when we start to go
The herons cry and climb as toward a home
In columned drafts between the Gulf and sun,
Alive in fiery light above the foam.
Bright heirs of an almost winterless domain,
They hear our voices rising as they glide
Higher in time's elation and declare
That time is but a flyway to the side
Of one who calls all creatures by their names,
His timbre their intention on the course.

William Mills

THE MEANING OF COYOTES

We were trying to get the rocks to speak
In northern Arizona.
Time stretched as far as we could work backward
With the pieces of yesterday
Sifted in our screens,
Left for us to interpret.
The Hopis left us only with hard things,
No song,
But the hafted point,
The killing intention
That ran before it like lightning
Now cooled in flint.

Strange the hunger we have
For the early ones,
Like hounds running their quarry's tracks backwards.

We sat by the fire in the long evening.

Suddenly off the dark mountainside
A coyote's yapping-howl
Stilled everything.
Another howl, answering
From the other side of the valley.
Whether they gathered to love
Or to kill,
They spoke to each other
And they spoke to us,
Taking us past the hafted point,
The song.

WATCH FOR THE FOX

He lit it more for the light and
Movement it gave
Than against the cold.
He had felt the old fear
Skulking like a fox
Around a hen house,
Patient,
Time on its side,
People sleep.
But a jerk inside
(something his fathers
 had passed on)
Said to get up,
Go deeper in darkness
And get something to burn,
See himself again and
Watch for the fox.
Watching, he knew
The fire
Defines
The fox.

Judith Moffett

CECROPIA TERZINE

I found one fall snugged tight onto its twig
A tapered swelling spun, a woven chamber
Milkweed-pod shapely, roughly half that big,

And like a pod which has by late September
Split open, spilt its cottonseeds and dried
To wrapping-paper lightness. Was this slumber?

A death? The chamber seemed unoccupied
And much unraveled at the tip, though shaken
It rattled as if *something* were inside—

A walnut in its hull . . . I'd touched the broken
Skyblue or speckled cups of songbird eggs
And shells of locusts, each a hollow icon

Still clinging to the bark with empty legs,
And loved their one-time tenants' winged completion;
And, knowing well what fragile sorts of dregs

Cicadas, sparrows, seeds leave, my impression
Of this cocoon's light dryness kept me quite
From seeing any signs of occupation.

And that was why, one January night,
I jerked awake for such a ghostly reason:
Somewhere I'd heard the thumping-flopping flight

Of wings shut up in darkness and in prison,
Doggedly feckless. Hangers crashed and clanged
Another terrifying diapason.

I lay a long time while the trapped wings banged
Themselves on wood and wire in their trouble
And blindly ricocheted and boomeranged

And flop-thumped till exhaustion wore them feeble
Inside the only closet in my room.
And when I switched a lamp on and felt able

To open it
        there toppled from the gloom
Heavily sideways, stunned by light, a glory
Huge as a plate, with tiny perfect plume-

Like new antennae, feet red-orange and furry,
Thick furry abdomen, each panting wing
Powdered with cocoa-colored plush and starry

With one rich eyespot. Months before the spring
My lamplit nights had brought him forth in splendor,
Mad with an urge that powered his battering:

Break free and find your mate O find her find her!
My windowsills lay inches deep in snow
The females meant for him were sleeping under.

Born out of season, twenty years ago.
The wasteful barren death of so much beauty
Should hurt me till my own. I've come to know

Too well since that cold night in Cincinnati
What barren is, and for my sorry crime
Begun to know a terror and a pity

Unsayable save through this keeping time,
These saving graces slanted rhyme and rhyme.

Elizabeth Seydel Morgan

THE ADAMSONS' PEACOCKS

Brakes screech, heavy metal thunks. A second, then glass crashes.
Behind my woods there's been another wreck on Three Chopt Road.

Waiting for the sirens makes me hear the silence,
And in that silence come uncanny human cries for help.

I've lived here long enough to know this cry
Is like, but only like, a woman's in the labor room,

Or a woman slammed against a wall with two hands on her shoulders
Who knows that what those hands do next will kill her in some way.

Help, oh, help, oh, help: the desperate aspirants of pain,
The long vowels of howling the long hours of the first birth.

Or the cry you tried to stifle, trying to be quiet, to hide
From someone—the parents, the children—the truest sound you make.

The way a peacock calls its mate: unseemly, raucous, screamed.
Like brakes too late, like any passion over the limit,

Beyond the gorgeous plumage, after the measured dancing,
Past any sequential ritual we ever learned.

FAMILY LIFE

$500 for a single poem with the theme of "family
bliss and failure"
      —contest announced in
        Poets & Writers Magazine, June, 1996

This—
brown-haired boy, ambling up a mountainside,
picking a tune on his banjo, his little daughter
making her own way on lamb's legs
through the thick April grass.
And they're mine: boy, baby, I
can even claim the framing:
air, sun, bluegrass tune, scent of pear tree
barely blooming, those pale green poplars
mending winter ridges.
This railing I am leaning on.
This woven moment
holding time
around me like a nest.
Bliss—
five hundred dollars is not enough
for me to tell the rest.

Robert Morgan

DOUBLE SPRINGS

I used to wonder how
two springs could issue from the hill
a yard apart. Why not dig deeper
and unite their flow?

And later realized they
surfaced close from opposite
directions. The southern
sweeter, though the northern's steady

effluence came cold, even in the dry
months when its neighbor
slacked and almost stood, with
algae thickening the edges.

In the church nearby I've heard
sermons on the trinity describe
their separate currents merging to
one branch. The sweet uneven

head rose from the hillside leaning toward
Dark Corner, while the constant
icy thread emerged
from the farm country. In summer

they condemned the slow one and
when I came down to drink before
or after preaching its partner sure
enough ran clear, with ebullition

dimpling the surface above the pores,
and purifying lizards gripped

the sandy floor. But after swilling
there I'd dip the gourd

into the slightly silty left
embellished now with leaves and spiders
and aquatic mosses for a richer sip.
That ungodly taste I'd carry home.

Lisel Mueller

PALINDROME

There is less difficulty—indeed, no logical difficulty
at all—in imagining two portions of the universe, say
two galaxies, in which time goes one way in one galaxy and
the opposite way in the other. . . . Intelligent beings in each galaxy
would regard their own time as "forward" and time in the other
galaxy as "backward."
    —Martin Gardner in *Scientific American*

Somewhere now she takes off the dress I am
putting on. It is evening in the antiworld
where she lives. She is forty-five years away
from her death, the hole which spit her out
into pain, impossible at first, later easing,
going, gone. She has unlearned much by now.
Her skin is firming, her memory sharpens,
her hair has grown glossy. She sees without glasses,
she falls in love easily. Her husband has lost his
shuffle, they laugh together. Their money shrinks,
but their ardor increases. Soon her second child
will be young enough to fight its way into her
body and change its life to monkey to frog to
tadpole to cluster of cells to tiny island to
nothing. She is making a list:
    Things I will need in the past
        lipstick
        shampoo
        transistor radio
        Sergeant Pepper
        acne cream
        5-year diary with a lock
She is eager, having heard about adolescent love
and the freedom of children. She wants to read

Crime and Punishment and ride on a roller coaster
without getting sick. I think of her as she will
be at fifteen, awkward, too serious. In the
mirror I see she uses her left hand to write,
her other to open a jar. By now our lives should
have crossed. Somewhere sometime we must have
passed one another like going and coming trains,
with both of us looking the other way.

MERCE CUNNINGHAM AND THE BIRDS

Last night I saw Merce Cunningham and his ten amazing dancers
dancing for eighty minutes without a break in the college gym.

I am trying to tell you how it was
            but of course there are no words
            for being wholly enclosed in a space,
            a tight cocoon without chinks
            so none of the wonder will leak out

Instead, I ask you to watch the assorted birds
feeding outside this window,
darting and dropping and zeroing in,
assuming positions in groups of threes
            or fours, to break up and form
            new patterns, other groups

how each incessant performer
signals a personal flash of color:
cardinal red, jay blue,
towhee orange, March pea green
            of not-yet-yellow goldfinch,
always tempered with black

how even their silences prefigure
shifts already known to the muscles

and how none leads or follows
how each moves
to the authority of its brain
its autonomous body

perpetual proof that the world

is energy, that to land
in a certain space at a certain time
is being alive; watch how they manage
to keep it up till each soul is fed

and disappear into nowhere

MISSING THE DEAD

I miss the old scrawl on the viaduct,
the crazily dancing red letters: BIRD LIVES.
It's gone now, the wall as clean as forgetting.
I go home and put on a record,
Charlie Parker Live at the Blue Note.
Each time I play it, months or years apart,
the music emerges more luminous;
I never listened so well before.

I wish my parents had been musicians
and left me themselves transformed into sound,
or that I could believe in the stars
as the radiant bodies of the dead.
Then I could stand in the dark, pointing out
my mother and father to all
who did not know them, how they shimmer,
how they keep getting brighter
as we keep moving toward each other.

LOSING MY SIGHT

I never knew that by August
the birds are practically silent,
only a twitter here and there.
Now I notice. Last spring
their noisiness taught me the difference
between screamers and whistlers and cooers
and O, the coloraturas.
I have already mastered
the subtlest pitches in our cat's
elegant Chinese. As the river
turns muddier before my eyes,
its sighs and little smacks
grow louder. Like a spy,
I pick up things indiscriminately:
the long approach of a truck,
car doors slammed in the dark,
the night life of animals—shrieks and hisses,
sex and plunder in the garage.
Tonight the crickets spread static
across the air, a continuous rope
of sound extended to me,
the perfect listener.

Marilyn Nelson

BALI HAI CALLS MAMA

As I was putting away the groceries
I'd spent the morning buying
for the week's meals I'd planned
around things the baby could eat,
things my husband would eat,
and things I should eat
because they aren't too fattening,
late on a Saturday afternoon
after flinging my coat on a chair
and wiping the baby's nose
while asking my husband
what he'd fed it for lunch
and whether
the medicine I'd brought for him
had made his cough improve,
wiping the baby's nose again,
checking its diaper,
stepping over the baby
who was reeling to and from
the bottom kitchen drawer
with pots, pans, and plastic cups,
occasionally clutching the hem of my skirt
and whining to be held,
I was half listening for the phone
which never rings for me
to ring for me
and someone's voice to say that
I could forget about handing back
my students' exams which I'd had for a week,
that I was right about *The Waste Land,*
that I'd been given a raise,
all the time wondering

how my sister was doing,
whatever happened to my old lover(s),
and why my husband wanted
a certain brand of toilet paper;
and wished I hadn't, but I'd bought
another fashion magazine that promised
to make me beautiful by Christmas,
and there wasn't room for the creamed corn
and every time I opened the refrigerator door
the baby rushed to grab whatever was on the bottom shelf
which meant I constantly had to wrestle
jars of its mushy food out of its sticky hands
and I stepped on the baby's hand and the baby was screaming
and I dropped the bag of cake flour I'd bought to make cookies with
and my husband rushed in to find out what was wrong because the baby
was drowning out the sound of the touchdown although I had scooped
it up and was holding it in my arms so its crying was inside
my head like an echo in a barrel and I was running cold water
on its hand while somewhere in the back of my mind wondering what
to say about *The Waste Land* and whether I could get away with putting
broccoli in a meatloaf when

suddenly through the window
came the wild cry of geese.

CHOSEN

Diverne wanted to die, that August night
his face hung over hers, a sweating moon.
She wished so hard, she killed part of her heart.

If she had died, her one begotten son,
her life's one light, would never have been born.
Pomp Atwood might have been another man:

born with a single race, another name.
Diverne might not have known the starburst joy
her son would give her. And the man who came

out of a twelve-room house and ran to her
close shack across three yards that night, to leap
onto her cornshuck pallet. Pomp was their

share of the future. And it wasn't rape.
In spite of her raw terror. And his whip.

LIKE FATHER, LIKE SON

It comes over him sometimes, he can't help
it, it just comes over him and makes him want
something, want to do something, something
naughty. Something bad. And whose god's gonna
grab his wrist and spank the back of his hand,
whose god's gonna shake him to tooth chatter,
slap his face snotty, say you fucking little
piece of shit. Whose god's gonna make him be good?
Whose god will see him tiptoe into a dark room,
sit on a fragrant narrow bed, touch a dimpled arm,
awaken the little secret, and let it come over him?
Whose god cares enough to stop him? Where was your
god when he needed one? He's a piece of shit,
all right. Child of the only goddamned god he knows.

HOW I DISCOVERED POETRY

It was like soul-kissing, the way the words
filled my mouth as Mrs. Purdy read from her desk.
All the other kids zoned an hour ahead to 3:15,

but Mrs. Purdy and I wandered lonely as clouds borne
by a breeze off Mount Parnassus. She must have seen
the darkest eyes in the room brim: The next day
she gave me a poem she'd chosen especially for me
to read to the all except for me white class.
She smiled when she told me to read it, smiled harder,
said oh yes I could. She smiled harder and harder
until I stood and opened my mouth to banjo playing
darkies, pickaninnies, disses and dats. When I finished
my classmates stared at the floor. We walked silent
to the buses, awed by the power of words.

Bink Noll

HOW IT FEELS ON A GOOD SATURDAY MORNING

The novel lies on the two pages
where I left it downward yesterday.
Nothing is more important—or less—
than the smell of this room, bed still unmade
where, the moment I step back in,
I come upon myself
in the entire complex of smells.
I lift the shades, turn off the bedside lamp.
Light and the sidewalks are established.
Good. Everything else is finished:
   breakfast, teeth, errands.
Nobody else needs to be phoned.
I lie down, my shoes on the sheets.
That is, I half-lie, my head against
the wooden headboard, the carved bumps of which
are familiar to the back of my head.
Just as this room has all these pieces—
from family, by choice / not much that's new—
my mind is furnished.
   It feels its own comfort.
The wallpaint, the waxed floor,
the white window frames: they may endure
invisible change but without regret.
I pick up the story to read.
Through this morning as if through my lifetime
the genial world pends, without incident
   except a fly
lands on the back of my hand
making a cold disc there.
I have begun to read.

Joyce Carol Oates

ABANDONED AIRFIELD, 1977

for my father, Frederick

In grass the cinder runways are hidden:
in grasses taller than children.
Nothing springs into movement but there is motion
          on all sides—
the shadows of low-flying planes
thinning to the shadows of starlings—
the trembling of pollen, the iridescence of black flies.
Above the corrugated roof a wind-sock flutters
          in gray shreds.
Thirty years. Thirty-five years.

Today's winds come from all directions.

Though it is Sunday there are no piper cubs circling
          to land,
there are no cars parked in the lot,
there are no children screaming with excitement
as their fathers test the sky.
The day's flying is over. It is nearly dusk.
The lightweight planes have dipped and soared and plunged
and fallen and righted themselves and risen and skimmed
low over that line of willows by the creek:
they have prepared soberly to land to taxi along the runway
to slow to come to rest to lie in broken rusted hulks.
The air-field is empty. The pilots sleep.
Exhausted, they feel the winds blow over them,
the grasses waving languidly above their heads.

Strange children have broken into the hangar,
have wrenched a door off its hinges.

Strange to us, the smears of tar and the smashed glass
and the small droning winds.
Who are we to survive those clumsy flights?
To recall the jarring thud of the plane's wheels
and the rightness of the cindery earth
and the sunburnt alarm of children who must witness
their fathers riding the air,
garish and frail as kites?

Now the field belongs to starlings.
Irritated by our presence they rise squawking
where gravity tosses them
and we cannot follow.

THE SUICIDE

didn't thank
didn't wave goodbye
didn't flutter the air with kisses
a mound of gifts unwrapped
bed unmade
no appetite

always elsewhere

though it was raining elsewhere
though strangers peopled the streets
though we at home slaved and
baked and wept and
hung ornaments
and perfumed the dark
did he marvel
did he thank

was he grateful   did he know
was he human
was he there

always elsewhere:
didn't thank
didn't kiss
toothbrush stiffened with unuse
puppy whining in the hall
car battery dead
sweaters unraveled

was that human?

Went where?

VISIONARY ADVENTURES OF A WILD DOG PACK

Snow-stubbled January fields and evil
frozen between our toes
by the time you see us
it is already too late
we trot across the vegetable world
in a pack of mad teeth and tongues

Voices in you speak
to our furious sorrow
we hear nothing
we are worm-ridden
bullet-shy
starving-crafty
we lap at pools of Arctic cold
we devour garbage
teeth and tongues and rib-rippling sides

Look:
a pack of stomachs covered in snarled fur!

Once over-loved we are now displaced
last summer's pets abandoned
by the roadside
not even lonely now
but forgetful of our old names
grunting and whining and squealing
a pack of stomachs roused at dusk
tongues aslant in stained mouths

We look like laughter, don't we?
tearing these feathery things apart
flinging the blood into the air
we charge in a pack
we whine and dodge and flee
savage-sad
wise mouths and guts
over-leaping our pet names
over-leaping the love
of our masters

FAMILY

What are we doing here jumbled
smelling of dust in a potato
sack? What is this dance we perform
sitting down? Tell me what are our faces
meant to declare, mashed together nose
against nose in friendly terror?

What is that word stamped faintly
on your forehead?—reversed blue ink
of an A & P melon? Oh in this crowd
it's a chore to breathe   to thrust a fist
through the bag to the dark
quiet cupboard—

Do we need so many elbows? so many
eyes crossing? Names leaping from mouths?

Why is it necessary to embrace
to make room? necessary to flatten the face
of stubborn signs? Why is the dance a jumble
of buttocks and calves
fingertips and eyelashes and stinging molecules
of sweat?

What are we doing here jumbled
for decades sharing the ache
of our dark back teeth? What is
the purpose of the dance? How does this
cupboard door unlock? Who has tied us
in here together and walked away?

Carole Simmons Oles

DAY TEN AFTER
HEART SURGERY,
SIGNING A CHECK

Bending forward on ratchets
as if she might again break
open breastbone to navel
or spring the ribcage
they had to saw through
to make good the heart inside

my mother signs on the correct line
an alien name—
like hers, but with consonants doubled
m's and n's drunk on their rises
like a needle stuck
loving one note

and I don't want to hear it
but I'm afraid of picking the arm up,
scratching the record.
I point, fetch her other glasses
and still the letters convene
too fast for her to grasp.

Seventy years ago
in the one-room schoolhouse
she learned words,
carried her name over snowdrifts,
gave it shining back
to her mother and father, earth-turners.

Now she must sign again
I say, banks are skeptics.

My breath climbs each extra curve
while we try to stay calm.
For this teaching, nothing
prepares me, nor for her
I'm so stupid

until here surfaces Miss Covell
who drilled me in penmanship.
Slow, I say. *Go slow, and count each hill*

as alive, beside me, needing cash
my mother signs her name.

Brenda Marie Osbey

FOR CHARLES H. ROWELL, ON THE DEATH OF HIS FATHER

I.

go tell them i have laid down my yard shoes
my house keys, my dead wife's handkerchief box
and the sight of my children
leaning at my face
in old photographs on the livingroom walls
and their voices saying
it was then
i saw it
he was with me in the field
we saw the brown dust when it covered the evening
all of these things:
i have laid them all by.

they are mourning me
and i am still a living man.

2.

my father stood in the field that evening
sifting the brown earth
through his turned-up fingers.
walking a little behind him
i was going through words in my head
testing how they sounded
in the empty expanse of the land.
he said something about a nephew
nathan or somebody.
i pulled on my cigarette
and watched him stretch his arm

across my line of vision
motioning over the field.

3.
my mouth is a barren plot of ground
a sand-colored silence
where my children stand hollow
over breakfast
two rooms away.
they discuss their mother
and the color of my urine.
they make these little sounds
eruptions i am not yet used to.
my death is in their throats and lungs.
they swallow hard before entering my bedroom.
my used body parts
are already in the grave.
i wonder can they see
how my soul is a grey fog
creeping the fertile land outside this window
to the left of the house?
but they want me to say something
because all my life
my name has been josiah.

4.
it is over now.
people are calling me long-distance.
writing on postcards
telling me how best to grieve.
they do not know that the young do not mourn.
they do not know that my hands are empty buckets
easily weighted to the ground with such stones.
they see me move both feet in succession
and rub my back with funeral lore.
etherine sings about *sweet peace.*
the others say *yes*

and talk of *going on.*
but then,
they have never seen the brown dustclouds
rolling over the rich alabama soil
on my daddy's land.

FAUBOURG

the faubourg is a city within the larger city
and the women walk in pairs and clusters
moving along the slave-bricked streets
wearing print dresses
carrying parcels
on their hips or heads.

within the small city of the faubourg
there is always work to be done:
rooms and yards and laundry to see to
and always some trouble
to be put to rest.
burdens to be shifted
from an arm to a hip
from a hip to the head.
there are children to be scolded and sung to.
there are wares to call out
to sell or buy or search for at market.
and along the narrow banqettes leading there—
a cook
a seamstress
a day's-work-woman to find or be found.
there are chickens to feel and buy
and get their necks wrung.
palm oil to buy and sell
palm wine
hot sweet potato pies.

and there are blues to be sung or heard
above the trees and rooftops
all hours of the day and night.

the dead must be mourned and sung over
and prayers told them to carry to the other side.
the dead must be chanted and marched to their tombs
and the tombs then tended and the dogs kept away.
yatta leaves must be dried and woven into belts and baskets.
rags must be burned in sulphur to ward off mosquitoes
and slave brick crushed and scrubbed across doorways.
there is love to be made
conju to be worked.

and quiet as it is kept
most anything can be done in the faubourg.

in such a city
what name is good for a woman?
in such a city
what good is any woman's name?

Sue Owen

CRICKETS

Some summer nights you
can hear them getting all
worked up over this idea
of cheerfulness and song.

Deep in the grasses where
they hide, there is a need
to be heard in the darkness,
even if their voices are

so small they sound
like a door creaking on
its hinge, or the squeak
a drawer makes when

it opens up at last.
It seems as if the damp
air and dew are trying
to hold their song down

out of sheer gravity,
but neither dampness nor
darkness makes them stop.
In fact, the crickets like

to show off their song,
to let it lift up off
the earth the way that
all notes rise to the stars,

and float up through the
thick night, as if their
joy itself were the only
light we needed to follow.

Anthony Petrosky

LISTENING TO MY SON'S HEART

It's a game we play.
Well, as much a game as I can play with a one-year-old.
It goes like this.
When I come home from work,
he's there, toddling around the kitchen, wide-eyed
in his baby blue sleeping suit
with the padded feet.
When he sees me, he smiles, and I do too,
and I imagine the sound, the *thud thud thud*
of his tiny heart that I remember
from the last time we played our game.
I stoop down so my haunches almost touch the floor
and open my arms for a hug. He walks over
in his confident but uneasy way
and we are eye to eye when he breaks into laughter,
wraps his arms around my neck, and gently
nibbles on my shoulder. I do the same,
and it's then that I hear it, his heart
much faster than mine. After a minute or so
he turns around and walks out of my arms
only to turn around again and walk back,
laughing, anticipating the hug
and, I think, the repetition. And again
I hear his heart, and again, momentarily,
an uncanny mixture of joy and fear,
happiness and anxiety overtakes me.
It is, I know, my pleasure in his life,
in his being here with us, and my fear
for him, for the difficulties yet to come.
But it is, also, a kind of self-pity;
the comfort of remorse that comes from imagining pain
juxtaposed against happiness, the permutations

of the future against the immediacy of the present,
the sound of his heart against the absence of it.

GOODBYE ON THE WIND

The sadness is coming again,
at first it was on the wind speaking to the night,
hushed, slightly crazed, an inconspicuous middle-aged
man babbling quietly into the darkness, into the empty,
closed faces, into the trees and buses, into the small
nooks and crannies of my lover's face and arms and belly,
and then when it was done, played out, left imperceptible,
overridden by business, by telephone calls and memos
and letters, by children running through the house with
footballs and music-boxes, it came raging down the street
on eighteen wheels, all chrome grill work, Peterbilt, the
biggest and most beautiful sadness, the one all mine,
enormous yet private, barreling headlong into every face
and job and conversation, hauling itself, hauling the sadness,
the leaving, the time closing down between her presence
and absence, the space between two bodies
in an embrace moving apart, the nostalgia and longing,
the lines in my old father's face, the sad ones, the frown
lines, the permanent traces that are becoming mine,
the cheap pleasures of such expensive sadness.
The old Jew, Heime—the one who carved meat,
who carried my father home, who buried his wife
and two sons, his father and mother, the carcasses
of bulls and children—wallowed in his sadnesses,
taught his eyes to droop and his face to hang in
a complete pitiful pout, and so did my mother
who froze her lovely round face into a stiff smile,
into a phoney cheerfulness, while all along harboring
inside of her the small sadness fire, living off of it,
begging it to keep her warm because it was all she had,

but my son who turns so intensely sad with his body,
with his folding-over-self suddenly throws it out,
like a ball, and runs up the stairs evading the bombs
and landmines, whistling or singing. Oh God, I feel
like wailing, like moaning along with the old women
sitting Shiva at my grandfather's funeral, I feel like
yelling out, like crying "don't go, you can't leave,
oh God I'm going to miss you," but I can't, but I
won't because the Dow goes up and down like
a rollercoaster, because the kids need a lunch
every day, because wars start and finish,
because the rain is always wet except
in the dreams, because there's no choice but
to embrace the sadness, to speak and walk
with it into the days and nights, because anyone
with an ounce of brains and experience knows
that distance is both a maker and undoer,
a magician of unpredictable and unequaled powers,
and you take what you get, and do what has to be done,
and all the other clichés of getting by.

Stanley Plumly

WALKING OUT

I would walk out of this flesh,
leave the whole body of my bones.
If I could I would undress utterly.

I would be silence: Even the sleeves
of my best coat would not know me.
I would write my name in cold blood

by a candle whose flame would fire
air, breath, everything, including paper.
I would be totally absent from myself,

from thought of myself; I would forget
myself entirely. I would go out only
at night, naked and perpetually catching

cold, and in fear of footprints, walk
on my hands. They would think *five-toed bird*
and at the edge of water imagine flight.

But I would still be walking, if I could,
out of body, leaving behind, in a wake
of absence, clothes, fingerprints, words.

NOW THAT MY FATHER
LIES DOWN BESIDE ME

We lie in that other darkness, ourselves.
There is less than the width of my left hand

between us. I can barely breathe,
but the light breathes easily,
wind on water across our two still bodies.

I cannot even turn to see him.
I would not touch him. Nor would I lift
my arm into the crescent of a moon.
(There is no star in the sky of this room,
only the light fashioning fish along the walls.
They swim and swallow one another.)

I dream we lie under water,
caught in our own sure drift.
A window, white shadow, trembles over us.
Light breaks into a moving circle.
He would not speak and I would not touch him.

It is an ocean under here.
Whatever two we were, we become
one falling body, one breath. Night lies down
at the sleeping center—no fish, no shadow,
no single, turning light. And I would not touch him
who lies deeper in the drifting dark than life.

Deborah Pope

LEAVING

I was waiting for you
at the end of the long
gravel road that wound
through the woods,
the house barely visible
back in the trees,
two windows lit
and balancing
November's early dark.
Walking out, I had watched
a sky turning from bone
to ash to black.
I had money and night
things stuffed in my bag,
I hoped you would see me
in the headlights.
A soft rain began.
It fell on the shoulders
of my upturned coat,
wet my face, my hair,
I could hear it falling
through the tough, hard
oaks and beeches,
the late autumn leaves
still stubborn on the trees,
sounding like birdshot,
or grains of sand
steadily, finely pouring.
And I thought suddenly
how I wanted to forget you,
forget everything,
that moment

go utterly blank,
so that I could
come back
and remember it
all from the start
to that waiting,
alone in the fresh,
cold night
and the rain
ticking, ticking.

PASSAGE

The emptying moon tips
just above the treeline.
We are the only car on the road.
So dark the night, so close
the line of trees,
it is as if we had gone

under the earth, or the ill-
colored wick of moon was
the lantern astern on a ship
that had cut us adrift.
We move in another dimension.
Moths swim up in our headlights

like ghost fish darting
in black water. The silence
of acceptance or calamity
seeps through the glass.
Already your knuckles
look like coral on the wheel.

The children sleep in shapes
they will settle to in time

on the ocean floor, their bones
uncollected, like a necklace
broken in the sand.
What did any of it come to?

The only light is what
we carry with us.
There is salt in my kiss.

Bin Ramke

TURNING FORTY IN DENVER

I wonder what they think, women, of men's
obsession with breasts, our tendency
to touch and wonder, to watch and wait

while they dress for work, hurried
in the morning, and lean into their clothes
as if it were merely biology bulging there.

I dream of such shapes while walking,
geometer of desire, desultory to work.
Churlish child of my own passion,

I watch the arc of mountains through mist
above the bundle of the city and think
of textures, a torrent of tactile fallings

down curved edges from eloquent tips
of rock and ice. The happy husband
has an indifferent wife amused

by his furious fondling, tolerant
of touch; meanwhile mothers mumble
into the nestled heads of small sons.

Julia Randall

A VALEDICTION

In the great shade of August, under the sycamores,
if it is hard to imagine Piedmont without trees,
think of Sahara, or the Hebrides.

Yet they are coming down,
the German woods, and templed Oregon;
deep in the Gros Ventre, and the Amazon,
the chain-saws buzz like locusts all day long.

Where did pollution enter: acid rain,
base power? Caryatids cannot keep;
the Law and Prophets smoulder on the heap
like California. We are left
whatever tinder memory can heft.
The very stuff of cells
forgets the fire, the glacier, the sea-swells,
sweet-breathing air, and finally ripe earth.
Nature and Liberty uphold a weight
like chastity—too grave, too great.

So poets enter, and forbid to mourn,
since by division we grew
into ourselves, and growing die,
still wanting our reunion
with earth or sea or sky. What planetary dust
made Cain the first contender for our meat,
saw Babylon and Rome fall out,
saw Donatello and Mozart? saw trees?
I shy at purposes,
and shrivelling, like the branch of Noah's dove,
praise passengers like leaves of love.

FOR THE KEEPER OF MSS

Earth was the first book, and the first pen
a stick or stone. Then color—was it blood
or mulberries? And then the medium
improved: papyrus, vellum.
How much the others aided our illumination.
Even yet
if not the quill, we dip
the bristle into vegetable dyes
and write the world before our eyes.

You have to scrape
the hair off, patiently,
for parchment, peel the eye,
too, to make sense of Noah's zoo,
or John's six-winged angel (and with twain
he flew). Or was it some other
evangelist, enisled in gold and blue
upon a page in some gray northern room
with ox and eagle, lion and man,
to cheer brocaded ladies at their hours
who had that vision?

Our eyes have histories
or how else should we look
upon Aeneas' or Iskander's book,
or spy upon the great
and gilded prospect of our first estate?
For all here's garden, where we fell
from fatal notice of the speaking tree,
and everywhere are flowers brilliantly
climbing the margins of our works and days;
even death and hell,
embowered in the codex and the scroll,
open our hearts like April promises.

And if such flowers on earth were never seen,
some keeper of the leaves has kept them ever green.

Barbara Ras

YOU CAN'T HAVE IT ALL

But you can have the fig tree and its fat leaves like clown hands
gloved with green. You can have the touch of a single eleven-year-old finger
on your cheek, waking you at one a.m. to say the hamster is back.
You can have the purr of the cat and the soulful look
of the black dog, the look that says, If I could I would bite
every sorrow until it fled, and when it is August,
you can have it August and abundantly so. You can have love,
though often it will be mysterious, like the white foam
that bubbles up at the top of the bean pot over the red kidneys
until you realize foam's twin is blood.
You can have the skin at the center between a man's legs,
so solid, so doll-like. You can have the life of the mind,
glowing occasionally in priestly vestments, never admitting pettiness,
never stooping to bribe the sullen guard who'll tell you
all roads narrow at the border.
You can speak a foreign language, sometimes,
and it can mean something. You can visit the marker on the grave
where your father wept openly. You can't bring back the dead,
but you can have the words *forgive* and *forget* hold hands
as if they meant to spend a lifetime together. And you can be grateful
for makeup, the way it kisses your face, half spice, half amnesia, grateful
for Mozart, his many notes racing one another toward joy, for towels
sucking up the drops on your clean skin, and for deeper thirsts,
for passion fruit, for saliva. You can have the dream,
the dream of Egypt, the horses of Egypt and you riding in the hot sand.
You can have your grandfather sitting on the side of your bed,
at least for a while, you can have clouds and letters, the leaping
of distances, and Indian food with yellow sauce like sunrise.
You can't count on grace to pick you out of a crowd,
but here is your friend to teach you how to high jump,
how to throw yourself over the bar, backwards,
until you learn about love, about sweet surrender,

and here are periwinkles, buses that kneel, farms in the mind
as real as Africa. And when adulthood fails you,
you can still summon the memory of the black swan on the pond
of your childhood, the rye bread with peanut butter and bananas
your grandmother gave you while the rest of the family slept.
There is the voice you can still summon at will, like your mother's,
it will always whisper, you can't have it all,
but there is this.

Jan Richman

HELLS

Everyone has gone through hell, that's
what I love about the world. Even dentists,
and the couple in the convertible thrilling
Central Park West, winter lights landing
like spacecraft on their hair. In the dark
under the dashboard, their shoes
pinch their feet unflaggingly.
Babies knew hell, and judges, and Merlin, and nuns,
especially nuns. There is the hell of the loyal
fan, the hell of the germ, and of the arm
that reached so far across the fence
that it's become the fence. Just think
of the not-yet-born, those poor wanderers
without organs or bills of health to fear for,
scouting out the helicopter with its rhythmic slashes.
Sometimes I rejoice when my body greets me
at the corner, saying Hello I'll be your ride
home tonight, and I aim for the wig
of that body talking, gratefully climb
into its pathetic skin, as into
the consolation of the specific.

Paulette Roeske

THE BODY CAN ASCEND
NO HIGHER

Capuchin Catacombs, Palermo

Hung up on hooks,
they lean from their niches, these thousands,
each with something to show—
top hat, Count Dracula cloak,
Jesus beard, two blue eyes
dry as eggs. Someone
has planned this party,
rigged the monk with a broomstick spine,
the bride with breasts of straw.
In a high alcove, an unascribable breeze
lifts the veil from a seventeenth-century face
that mocks the old promise: *dust to dust.*

But how they tire of the dry
preserving air, immovable hand
falling short of what itch, the generations
trooping past arrayed in the dress of the times—
those mirrors they stare back at,
showing how the world has not changed,
chaining them to their lives
as they would have led them.

WORDS FOR UNACCOMPANIED VOICE AT DUNMORE HEAD

One old friend who never writes me tells another:
The boy has need of lyrical friends around him.
Don't ask me how I ever found that out,

Given as I am to these fugitive headlands
Where not so long ago the news from Dublin
Arrived washed up with driftwood from the States,

Where the gulls rehearse the local word for weather
And then free-fall through ragged clouds to the sea wrack.
The bar at the end of the world is three miles east.

Last night the music there ascended with the smoke
From a turf fire and showered down in dying sparks
That fell on lovers and the lonely ones alike

Where they cycled the dark roads home or lingered
By a bridge till every cottage light was out—
Fell silent from the night as innocent as milkweed.

All night those soft stars burned in my watchful sleep.
At dawn I abandoned my rackety faithless car
To its own persuasions, took up a stick

And leaned uphill into the wind for the summit.
No music here but the raw alarms of seabirds
And the tireless water high against the cliff face.

No more the flute and the whiskeyed tenor rising,
The chorus of faces in the drift of smoke.
This is the rock where solitude scrapes its keel

And listens into the light for an echo.
This has to be good practice for that last
Cold wave of emptiness on whatever shore,

But why do the reckoners in my nightmares
Never ask me what I said to the speechless
Assembly of whitecaps instead of was

There anyone arm-in-arm with me as I spoke?

WAITING FOR YOU WITH THE SWALLOWS

I was waiting for you
Where the four lanes wander
Into a city street,
Listening to the freight
Train's whistle and thunder
Come racketing through,

And I saw beyond black
Empty branches the light
Turn swiftly to a flurry
Of wingbeats in a hurry
For nowhere but the flight
From steeple-top and back

To steeple-top again.
I thought of how the quick
Hair shadows your lit face
Till laughter in your voice
Awoke and brought me back
And you stepped from the train.

I was waiting for you
Not a little too long

To learn what swallows said
Darkening overhead:
When we had time, we sang.
After we sang, we flew.

R. M. Ryan

AFTER THE WORST IS KNOWN

Now is not the time
for the tall words
in their startling clothes.

No more will be said
of what the gnats mean
gathering

to disappear.
The woods are closed,
the season of allegory

done. Instead
rattle off your list
of where you'll go

and what you'll do
as if you really will
survive.

That much they'll understand,
the ones
who go on planning

new ways to exchange
fives for ones
and ones for fives

while at night
keep meeting
what isn't true—

the man in feathers
bowed down by gravity
reading by a fire

in the Book of Hieroglyphs
of shapes like water
in words like air.

Stephen Sandy

THE WATER SPIDER

Dilatory cormorants, airing their heavy wings
like paltry aliens in capes, look shoreward
as mist burns upward, taking emerging landfall
in stride, sunlight skidding among their wings
                    spreading, unspreading.

Low tide, the sluggish ledges surface from the cove;
raw, dour and putrid, slick from the deep,
stray shards of Arnold's naked shingle: yet
a minor eminence above the tide supports
                    a rod of grass—

enough to be owned, but not enough to have
a name. The weedy brows come up for hours;
they belong to Mrs Thompson while they're topside—
to be seen or stepped on. But how they are rooted, how
                    their tentacular

huddle of shelves lies in wait to lunge at a keel!
Men who warily skirt them from wharf to mooring
have wished them gone; lurking or gleaming, minimal
black alp at morning's neap or slant garden
                    of kelp and fucus

tossing awash as if to beckon, beckon
the dinghy's prow as it skates barely over them;
rising or resting inches below our keel.
Yet sunny mornings in July this year a launch
                    will cautiously put

one passenger ashore, a lady in a smock
and broadbrimmed hat, who carries her stool,

her case of water colors; sets her parasol
and settles in to sketch sky, cove, pine-hedged
                    granitic banks.

The cormorants, black adjutants, back off
but seem to follow every move of brush on pad
where water sways and calms and with the hours
mounts toward her place. As slabs of ledge dry off
                    in the sun she spreads

her sketches on the rocks to air, weighting them down
with loosened stones. She keeps on painting. Makes
her way down to the water to sketch a rock pool
and the water spider that makes its lobed shadow
                    fringed with colors

flash on the sunny bottom as it wins
its way grassward from cold eddies. Each day
a novelty, as out of mist rocks abruptly loom,
although from habit sailor or lobsterman knows
                    which way to head

having a sense of what he's aiming for, knowing
the way to miss this obstacle—inert, succinct,
not veined or crystal-flecked but black as any
ruin charred—only an elderly sketcher's
                    destination.

GROUNDS

Think about the positive
and negative space. Think about big
a little. Think about your relationship to the object.
Think of vast space, and intimate.
Think about the light being warm—or cool.
About shadows and the light which makes them

and if they are blue
or only pictured that way. Think about narration
and composition. Telling a story and how the scale
will come along with the tale.
Think about interpretation about
what Peter was going to say, what Paul said,

the history this is
and the language it is of;
about paint and slides, the lingo
of color, the lingo of paint, the lingo.
Think about thinking, listen up
to the ceiling, figured, grounded.

Herbert Scott

THE WOMAN WHO LOVES OLD MEN

She loves the brown moles
widening to pools of oil
on their faces, their eyes
turning to milk, the tiny
forests of their ears;

and the shoulders,
wearing thin as skulls,
the slow glaciers of flesh
sliding from bone;

and oh the white bellies,
the pure salt of their bellies,
she could bury her face forever
in such perfect snow.

Yes, she marries them,
and they roost in her arms
like tired birds as she listens
for the last drawn croak
before that certain stillness.

And they, thankful, never know
it is their deaths she loves,
their bodies she lays out
like polished wood, as she dreams
of the one who will marry her twice.

James Seay

THE PURITAN

in response to the statue by Saint-Gaudens

Wee must be knitt together
John Winthrop preached in purest metaphor

to those aboard the Puritan ship
Arbella, word and vision sure as apocalypse.

And that is what is easy to ignore,
looking at Saint-Gaudens' foursquare,

embronzed, and square-toed monument to dourness:
how their sense

of social covenant
informed so much of what we meant,

how intensely it was community,
and how by only sternest Liberty

in their narrow town
could we parlay the toehold of taken ground

into what we now call home.
Hawthorne spoke of a lamp

of zeal within their hearts, enriching all
with its radiance, and all was well

until the lamp began to dim
and then we saw their system,

how hard, cold, and confined it was,
he said, who surely knew them best.

In his tale "The May-Pole
of Merry Mount," you will recall

that iron Endicott
orders cropped the locks

of the bridegroom's hair who had gaily danced and wed
the Lady of the May. Even the trees turn sad.

But what invariably saddens me more
is when they shoot the dancing bear,

Puritans bent
on killing any merriment,

grim in their iron armor;
hard toil, he wrote, . . . *sermon and psalm, forever.*

Tell me, though, why do I pause
in the steadfast contractual gaze

of this bronze Puritan that Saint-Gaudens
casts before us, pilgrims?—

this early one who looks across the years
and makes discretion clear.

Too rigid still,
his sense of evil,

but of common cause his sense is firm,
what's now being knit into our fabric as a blur.

DEEP IN DORDOGNE

There is a human cave
I once inhabited
for part of a morning
on a limestone bluff
deep in Dordogne.
Other rooms were vacant
in the town far below
at the Hôtel Cro-Magnon,
but I wanted to sit on the racial floor
where our home had been of necessity
both hearth and window in one.
I wanted to look out over the river
where game once came to water
and fish swam
toward our earliest tables.
When we were barely lingual
there was a view
to the edgy tree line
of holm oak and walnut,
and I tried to imagine fear and need
so deep I would dig into rock
with nothing but another rock
and then rest and bring fire
from below and eat
what I gathered and reach up higher
to begin another cave above
this, to chip away again with my rock
toward what I hoped
would be a safer, higher loft,
toward architecture and furniture,
toward mathematics and an instrument
for my song.
But another form like mine
is coming from beneath the understory
of oak and nut tree,
and I must decide if he can climb

with his club to my room,
and for what:
my food, my fur of aurochs,
my daughter he has tracked
with his one syllable?
Or to hear these words
I am working toward song?

DYLAN THOMAS IN INDIANA

The great giant is dead. Dylan dead.
Sheltered from a Paris rain I read a yellow handbill
On a bookstore window lighted by streetlight flames—

And the widow and the flaxen children
Will be grateful for anything at all . . .

And I remember first he pinched a lady's bottom
In Indiana moonlight while a party—liquidly literary—
Spored, whorled in the woodsy cabin.
Afterwards he humped his elbows on a camper's table
And gazing through screenwire on a backporch
Saw corn growing under an Indiana moon.

We chattered over the rough boards a radio script,
The crinkle-haired poet bombing with me
Bad, made-up lines across the table.
Resonant beyond belief he became
Southern planter, Negro slave running away, was a
Chicago gangster as I sweated more American grotesques
To feed all hot his ravenous maw—
Corn all around and upstairs the lady
In a maiden's pout swore and swore—
I remember her words to our giant,
"The rest of them treat you like God.
I'll be damned if I will."

And now in night of Parisian rain and flickering flame
I see my own eyes in the glass, my lips twisting out
The words that Death, a holy maiden pouting,
Had irrevocably etched
Like acid eating

Like white snakes coiling
Across the kinky head and pulpy pied face of Dylan
"The rest of them treat you like God.
I'll be damned if I will."

Sean Siobhan

SEVEN PIECES OF ADVICE

for Marnie

When conversing with a fool,
Say nothing smart; there is no need.

When conversing with a tree,
Say nothing wise; there is no need.

When you receive the gift of air,
Say your thanks.

When you are beaten by the wind,
Bow your head.

When you catch another's hand,
Recall the hand is quicker than the heart.

When you catch another's heart,
Know the heart is quicker than the hand.

If the sun winks at you,
Wink back.

David R. Slavitt

SOLSTICE

A ghost of a sun flees from the sky as I,
the son of a ghostly father, hurry—to keep
blood circulating in the cold—to buy
another Yahrzeit candle in its cheap
glass I'll use for juice. I don't believe
in any of this, but he did, and I'd rather
feel like a fool than a bum. To think, to grieve,
to remember isn't enough. One must go to the bother
of doing something. Parents and children trade
places after awhile. I learned to endure
the whims, and accommodate to demands he made,
as he had done for mine once. Fewer and fewer
remain except for this minimal annual task.
A postcard comes from the people who did the stone
that marks the grave, so I don't have to ask
what date the Hebrew lunacy falls on.
They put it to me: will I refuse to do
what I know he would have wanted? I give in,
go out, come back again, still wanting to
earn praise as the good boy I've never been.
And when the sun has given up, I give
lip service, mumble the prayer, and light the wick.
It's guaranteed that the little flame will live
the whole twenty-four hours, which seems a trick
for two and three-quarter ounces of parafin.
All night shadows will dance on the ceiling and play
on the walls. And as I pass, I will glance in
to see how it's doing during the next day.
The flame is life, but the candle's guttering is
a reenacting of the death. I take
small satisfaction in my bearing this
as well as I do. I know it's for my sake

as much as his that I do this. My eyes brim,
but that can happen at the movies. Say
rather that I've bargained once more with him
and done what he wanted, only to keep him at bay.

SENTENCE

The bread was stale, her father explained—no good.
Sixteen months old, she considered this,
processed the information, and then announced,
"Eat bread, duck-ducks," referring to mallards
that scrounge on the pond in the college garden they visit,
my daughter, son-in-law, and she, my daughter's
daughter. A rather Latinate trick, to hold
in suspense her emphatic subject, but she will learn
handier ways to modulate and stress.
Still, her meaning was clear and clearly beyond
the first business of pointing, of sticking labels
to objects: baba (bottle); bow-bow (dog);
or baby. Better and better articulating,
clarifying like cloudy tap water that stands,
there were nouns first and, later, modifiers:
"Elena's book," or simply a "blue hat."
But this is something new and utterly other,
with subject, verb, and object dancing now
behind her glittering eyes. It is not the wrath
of Achilles, or man's first disobedience and
the fruit of that forbidden tree, not yet,
but it's what she needs in order for them to happen.
Call it the plain the citadel looks out on,
or the empty sea beyond at which they stared,
shielding their eyes for their first glimpse of a mighty
armada rumor had said was on its way.

ADAM

> Two Paradises 'twere in one
> to live in Paradise alone.
> —Andrew Marvell

So Adam is naming the creatures, the bull and the cow, and the ram and the
  ewe, and the horse and the mare, and the rooster and the hen, and the
  drake and the duck, and after a while he begins to understand the pattern
  of this and he looks up and asks:
"What about me? The 'man' and the 'what'? How is it that only I do not
  have a mate and that I am the only one for whom there is not a female of
  my kind?"
This is not a surprise to the Lord, who has already thought to Himself: "It
  is not good for man to be alone," but He has done nothing about it, and
  the rabbis wonder why not, what could He possibly be contemplating?
There is a long silence in the study house and perhaps a fly buzzes at the
  window as the rabbis try to imagine what might have been in the divine
  mind, which means that they have to imagine themselves as wiser, larger,
  better, which is to say more generous, and at length the eldest of them,
  stroking his yellowing beard, suggests:
"Let us suppose that the Almighty, blessed be He, hesitated because He
  understood what was going to happen. He knew what Eve would do and
  knew that Adam would complain to Him. So He waited until Adam
  asked on his own, and only then, and with a heavy heart, He gave."
Now let us imagine the venerable rabbi getting up and opening the window
  so the fly can escape. But it is late in the season, and the rabbi knows that
  there is no escape and that the fly will die anyway.
Nobody says anything, because what is there to say?

CAUTION

There comes a time when you can bear no more,
some random scrap of news having proved to be
the straw that breaks your spirit's back. New York

has owls in every borough big enough
to take a good-sized cat? You feel their wings
beating the air over your head and resolve
   never to leave your house.

You recognize the rightness right away
of this avoidance of such pain and pity
as everywhere abound, but the sound of rubber
squealing on pavement, the silence, and then the smash
of glass and metal break into that tight circle
you've drawn. You draw it tighter, smaller, and promise
   never to go downstairs.

The feeling, nevertheless, persists of risk,
dreadful and universal. You don't quite trust
your mental status, but isn't that just another
proof, another worry? What can you do
but carry on somehow, as conquered countries
always have, and face it that you are likely
   never to leave your room.

With blankets drawn up to your neck, it should
be safe, but panic still takes your breath away.
Your heart races; you often break into the cold
sweats of the last judgment. The baseball bat
you keep within easy reach may be of some
use. There's no more retreat, now that you've sworn
   never to leave your bed.

Dave Smith

MAKING A STATEMENT

Thousands, lately, have asked me about my hair.
Why is it so long? Why haven't you cut it?
I think about Sampson, of course, and his woe.
His hair like thickets where I was born, swamps,
tall grasses bending with red-winged blackbirds
like a woman's nipples in the quick sun-gold.
I could tell about Sampson, about the girl,
but I say my head is cold. I need cover.
Playing tennis with a leggy blonde I love,
I admit I can't do anything with it, my youth.
She rolls her eyes into a smashing serve.
"You old guys," she sighs with her drop-shot.
Back and forth all day, yellow balls, long gray hair.

BOYS IN THE SQUARE AT BOLOGNA

Across the courtyard of gold fountains at dusk
they strut, water lifting like smoke from penises
of stone. The dark earth cools as each one
preens in the square's mouth, indolents, masks,
beringed fingers, pigeons cooing for secrets
of the centuries oozed like spilled milk.
When girls come in silky heel clicks, three
whistle the air's exotic cries. They bob
like fish white for the moon. Some disrobe,
chests pale as panties, big neckchains, amulets
dancing, Marlboros, scooters' razz. The loudest
spout louder what fucking they will do tonight,
their hands miming the untouched and ripe.

DESCENDING

Remember that tin-foil day at the beach descending
on water the color of slate, the man descending,
just a bald head like an emptied melon descending
God knows where, same day a shy girl-child descending
with doll and bike to darkness where, descending
the hill with dumptruck vizer down, sun descending,
a father squints just once and the years descending
ever now spin him like a pump's flush-pipe descending
to pure waters he can never reach and, descending,
what of wings flamed gold, dusk's holy glow descending,
heron, tattered, wearied, news-heavy head descending,
that's left by hunters to float all night, descending
as they do into sleep, the earth clean, just descending?
Where, and with whom, are those we've seen descending?

LUNCH

Hours of tapping keys and staring, sullen clouds
the morning's mood, all scud and bump, hold
and go, images of what's unknown, yet wanted
dissolving so the sun appears, the day yields.
The shade is cold but the courtyard's filled
with flume of light, the soul's warm surround
I bring my lunch to: Vienna bread homemade,
local cheese, its wedged hunks like marigolds
yellow and sharp, bologna's muscle added,
and mustard to make the eyes weep, and beer,
beaded Dutch, a fistful of chips, an orange
deftly sliced so, unbruised, inner light's let out.
Crows struggle with their rhymes. I eat, all ears.

R. T. Smith

PASSAGE TO KILRONIN

On the morning boat from Rossaveal
I listened to the outboard's knock
behind our dory creaking like coffinwood
and tugged my borrowed slicker snug
as a monk's cowl. As sea chop
and the odors of oil and salmon stunned
me, the boatman offered a flask
of brandy, saying it was a big day
for the Irish, World Cup soccer match,
the Republic against the North, but
a boy off one of the local trawlers had
been missing since dawn. I was dazzled
by sun flashing off the bow cleat
and every wavelet. I was out to study
vowels and isolation, the Gaelic
nouns not even Cromwell's henchmen
nor TV could root out. I was riding
the swell and luster to the ruins
of a language, but the sea's pitch
and wind said grief is the only dialect
that endures. I breathed shallow
and chatted about penalties and corner
kicks as the Arans rose like loaves
in the distance. Then we struck a zone
so calm we were spellbound to silence.
On the shore where water was unsinging
itself in the old tongue the boy's
soft body waited, wedged fast amid
the still and eloquent island stones.

Radcliffe Squires

THE GARDEN OF MEDUSA

for Caroline Gordon

You have the choice whether to go or not.

You will be seated at a table, perhaps,
On a headland. Other diners have gone.
The waiter has cleared his face like an abacus
And departed. The playful yachts
Have fled, and far beneath you the last
Child has left the beach where the sand
Is turning blue, and the fingering
Of land by sea ceases between
The ebb and the rising. You may ebb then;
Or rise, stand among cobalt bee orchises,
Then walk through the furze on the cliff edge,
Feeling birds start from their nests at
Your ankles. Your next step will have wind
For an instant under the descending toe
And rising heel, and you will come down,
When you come down, in her garden.

You will hear the dead-leaf rustle of serpents
And catch the odor of clay and cold violets.
You have another choice then. You may
Observe her in the dark mirror you will find
Has grown in the palm of your hand.
You can see there how the serpents churn,
Unravelling the cloth of the world.
Below them you will see eyes colder
Than tourmaline cast down toward lips
That have drawn all body's blood
Into themselves and, swollen, sweat blood

Through transparent skin.
If you carry this face in your mirror
Out of the garden you will defeat
Your enemies (though there will be no end of them).

You will make a notorious marriage,
And newspapers will tingle with the shock of your name.

Yet, there is another choice. You may look
About the garden where those who were turned
To stone still stand. How beautifully they
Have weathered. The grasp has run from the hands.
Frail honeycomb of limestone shows in the hollowed
Cheek. And the eyes, hardly eyes now,
More nearly birds' eggs nested in stone, are all
Turned calmly in the same direction. It is as if
Sunlight had broken through the roof of the
Underworld, and all the dead had forgotten
Their living sins as wind and rain moved on them.
You may, after all, choose to forget the mirror and
See what the face really looks like.

These are the choices, and none of them easy.

Richard Stansberger

DON'T MAKE FRIENDS
WITH THE DEAD

They end up coming over every morning,
with a flicker and pop
as soon as you step into the shower.

Then all day long you follow them around
asking questions like a dumb little brother.

They go from room to room for their own reasons.
Handel loves the soap operas and the way
the silver sounds when he dumps out the drawers.
Gogol is fascinated by the rock collection,
and Otto III studies the scrolls of light
unfolding on the floor.

But the dead bore easily, get blurry, and you
end up following them down the basement stairs
where they disappear through a back wall
and you suddenly notice your bare feet
cold in the dirt of the root cellar.

Timothy Steele

FOR MY MOTHER

Barton, Vermont

It was late August. Standing by the well,
I watched you gather wildflowers in the brake.
Red clover, goldenrod, and camomile,
The dragonflies and sunlight in the air—
And you waist-deep in all that color there.
So young, you seemed then. There was hay to make

And a cloud shadow on the Stevens' hill.
We two had grown apart, but I could see,
That moment, what you once were, and are still.
Only the light could touch you. The divorce,
Your father's death, the hard years: these, of course,
Were there, too. But your curiosity

And quiet were as wild as weeds, set off
From all the past. Mother, I know your ways:
Columbian prints; the mild defensive cough
You fill a silence with; that picnic ease,
Talk, and a paper plate poised on your knees.
Yet I was startled. Innocent of days,

How much of pain and learning we survive!
And I, discovering what I'd known before,
Stood silent in your calm, the light alive
And perfect as you finished your bouquet,
The wind and the long grass rippling away.
Nor did I call you. Nor could I ask more.

John Stone

HE MAKES A HOUSE CALL

Six, seven years ago
when you began to begin to faint
I painted your leg with iodine

threaded the artery
with the needle and then the tube
pumped your heart with dye enough

to see the valve
almost closed with stone.
We were both under pressure.

Today, in your garden,
kneeling under the sticky fig tree
for tomatoes

I keep remembering your blood.
Seven, it was. I was just
beginning to learn the heart

inside out.
Afterward, your surgery
and the precise valve of steel

and plastic that still pops and clicks
inside like a ping-pong ball.
I should try

chewing tobacco sometimes
if only to see how it tastes.
There is a trace of it at the corner

of your leathery smile
which insists that I see inside
the house: someone named Bill I'm supposed

to know; the royal plastic soldier
whose body fills with whiskey
and marches on a music box

How Dry I Am;
the illuminated 3-D Christ who turns
into Mary from different angles;

the watery basement,
the pills you take, the ivy
that may grow around the ceiling

if it must. Here, you
are in charge—of figs, beans,
tomatoes, life.

At the hospital, a thousand times
I have heard your heart valve open, close.
I know how clumsy it is.

But health is whatever works
and for as long. I keep thinking
of seven years without a faint

on my way to the car
loaded with vegetables
I keep thinking of seven years ago

when you bled in my hands like a saint.

DEATH

I have seen   come on
slowly as rust
sand

or suddenly   as when
someone leaving
a room

finds the doorknob
come loose in his hand

JANUARY: A FLIGHT OF BIRDS

Watching the birds, I think of Bach,
each of the distant wheeling flock

a black note on a turning page,
the darkened afternoon the stage.

Watching their wide, then narrow belt
I imagine how Bach felt,

with hundreds of melodies all at once,
inventing his own celestial stunts.

In their equivalent of cantata,
the birds perform a short fermata

then in silent sky-bound bugle
swoop and go, their music fugal.

I think of their flight in terms of Master
Bach at his keyboard, writing vaster

harmonies than the court could dream—
which is why, in pure esteem,

the world would be, if Bach- and bird-less,
as much diminished as if wordless.

THE BASS

Because I was 37 and he was 10
I was presumed and of course
to know everything important

plus
how to take the fish off the hook.
I'd been told largemouth

and striped bass
both   either
waited for us below

the still crystal of the lake
I had no expectation though
of actually catching a fish

when somehow we did
After we hauled it heavily
in over the gunwales

like a glittering glory
no way was I about to touch
that wide mouth, those razor fins

gills, those sparkling cold-blooded
scales
until all spasm stopped

To this day my son
may think the way
to take a fish off the hook

is to place it, hook still intact
in the bottom of the boat
place a paddle over the fish

and keep your foot gently but steadfastly
on the paddle on the fish
After the flailing and flopping

I managed with something like
experience to get the hook out
Then as morning broke over us

we made our slow electric way
back to the boathouse
That fish won for us

a trophy
which I keep here on my desk
to remind me of that morning and of

how unexpected the end may be
how hungry
how shining

Dabney Stuart

GLANCE

Light touched me where I was looming,
dusted the fibers; the shuttle moving
was like a needle through it,
stilled in it as I was stilled.

Before I thought I looked at the light,
its drift and penchant, my eyes loving,
but would have watched it in the threads
at my hand, had I been so skilled.

GRIEF

> It is the way into the self.
> —F. Nietzsche

It's a short road that goes on forever.
It makes a single turning.
I die traveling it, passing again
the few houses I have always passed,
filled with the same few people.
When I learn to speak of them
I discover I am alive
only in the speaking. What I know
as my self grows in the speaking,
but is only an echo when I talk
of anything else, or am silent.
It is an echo I hear sometimes,
but sometimes it's as far away
as my birth. The only way

to enter it is to speak again those words
I have learned from the few people
who are lost in my keeping.
They never speak.
They listen for the words
I have discovered where they live.
My trail is marked by the places
I have spoken, as by husks
of insects which have flown away.

MY BEST ROOM

> Good men ye be, to leave me my best room,
> Ev'n all my heart, and what is lodged there.
> —George Herbert

Usually today I walk
your former walks, turning
a word inside for you,
listening in the gray gym
while the mullions of the old
arched windows lower
their shadows on the guy wires,
as if they would sever
them and let the worn,
literal backboards sway
in their hanging drift.
What misplaced nostalgia keeps
them pending there? Or do people
just forget, when they get on
with it? Who comes here
besides me and the man who turns
the wide mop amiably from one end
of the floor to the other, making
and erasing tracks? I see

the antique set-shot fly,
your hands suspended,
the tips of your fingers
caught in the aimless
motes of dust in a slant
of sunlight. The band
on the parade ground,
muted at this distance, becomes
mostly tuba and drumbeat
for the resplendant corps.
Some officers still wear
sword and shako for these
ceremonial paces.
                              I've kept you
alive twenty-six years past
your dying. You'd think
I was trying to wear you
out, all that time, and now
I've brought you to this higher
air where I, too, get light-
headed, walking, and can't
catch my breath.
Neither of us
is at home here, on these windy
tracks. It never
rains, and the spare
piñon nettling the dry
wash are poor blown
dregs of our Shenandoah
woods. Still, you bear
me the same gift,
heightened, as always, by your
being gone. This year
from all the images I
could draw to celebrate
your birth, I see you
dance, which I never

saw. Simultaneously, you
glide on your stubby
legs across the polished
parquet of some country
club, and leap and click your heels
on the swirling mesa,
snapping your fingers, breathless,
full of yourself, of me being
full of yourself. Accompanying
your ebullience, the dust here
is the usual dust;
we borrow our shade
of it, lend it a spark, and pass.
Our ways leave us
where we are, words
following the long divide
where I continue, listening
for the air's implicit touch
on your open hands.

> to my father
> 11 October 1997
> Chaco Canyon, New Mexico

PALM READER

The end of my life
hops into my hand
like a grasshopper in a dry field.
If I were going to fish with it
I would close my hand
over it and place it in a jar
with some dry grass in the bottom
and air holes punched through the lid.
At dusk I would thread my hook
through its collar just behind

its curved black eye, or run the hook
up through its throat and out its mouth,
carrying a brown bubble on the tip.
Cast into the placid, twilit pool
it would twitch on the surface
as if it belonged there and could drift
until it reached the bank
and leapt back into the field
and into my hand again.
If I were simply curious
or gone into another phase where fishing
was a boyhood silhouette and my wrist
didn't remember the rod tip's
delicate motion, I would watch it
interrupt the lines in my palm:
vaguely reptilian with its yellow-
brown armor plating, the upper leg
chevronned, the lower with its rows
of fine barbs, thin as a needle.
It could be taken for a calm,
meditative vestige of another time,
or simply an insect terrified to poise
by this alien surface it's lighted on.
I could say it looks back at me.
If I could see with its eyes
I would become a mosaic of light
and shadow, colored in some way
complementing the background I seem
to emerge from, or blend with.
I would be as still and complex
as it is, and it would live in my hand.

Eleanor Ross Taylor

LAST ANT

They scutter in my dreams, the ants
that left the flower pot,
　　　that third plant
　　　I watched die, one of three
basils rescued from the freeze.
A fungus or mildew.
　　　I had to pull it up
　　　and leave the soil to dry.

Then ants began to come out,
cross the crater, the dusty
　　　desert of old potting soil;
　　　every appendage twitching, they explored
the great clay wall,
the width of plastic saucer,
　　　white longitude of sill,
mad for a jot to drink.
The natural thing to do was kill them all.

This morning, one more ant
ran wildly—he knew where?—
a straight line toward the sink.

Someone at the University
might take his questions:
　　　why there's no rainfall
　　　anymore, what happened to his
habitat, how Edens dry
up suddenly—in short, why
　　　he's endangered—things
　　　in his compound eyes not simple.

I gave the coup de grâce,
a little overkill (his bony suit)
      before I took the pot outside,
      and washed my hands.

Henry Taylor

BLACKBERRIES

On top of a ragged hill on the farm
Next to my father's, an old man
Sat on his front porch and reigned
Over a dominion of thistles and briars.

In his meadow, never mowed,
Blackberries grew wild, overran
The field, smothered the grass,
Bound the cows and ate them alive.

My sisters and I would steal
Under his fence, armed with pails,
To pick as many berries as we could.
We never got them all, hard as we tried.

One afternoon we stood in the briars
Reaching for berries over our heads,
Each one hanging before us like a bunch
Of grapes, when down from his porch

The old man tumbled, down the hill
Toward us, wild white hair in the wind,
Scattering all of his chickens as he ran.
His tiny dog yapped at his heels.

"Go back where you belong right now!"
And he waved his arms. We turned
And ran for the fence, clutching the pails
In our arms, scattering berries behind us.

We looked back once and saw him on the hill,
Shaking his fist in the wind and shouting.

"If you're too lazy to raise your own
Blackberries, by God, you shan't have mine!"

BERNARD AND SARAH

"Hang them where they'll do some good," my grandfather
said, as he placed the dusty photograph
in my father's hands. My father and I stared
at two old people posed stiffly side by side—
my great-great-great-grandparents, in the days
when photography was young, and they were not.
My father thought it out as we drove home.

Deciding that they might do the most good
somewhere out of sight, my father drove
a nail into the back wall of his closet;
they have hung there ever since, brought out
only on such occasions as the marriage
of one of his own children. "I think you ought
to know the stock you're joining with," he says.

Then back they go to the closet, where they hang
keeping their counsel until it is called for.
Yet, through walls, over miles of fields and woods
that flourish still around the farm they cleared,
their eyes light up the closet of my brain
to draw me toward the place I started from,
and when I have come home, they take me in.

THE MUSE ONCE MORE

    I take the air, the sun,
my ease, letting things go for a while, as the dog

blunders from my feet to the curb and back.
The words in the book I am holding recede,
waver into illegibility; the air
    trembles with jet planes, birds invade;
        it is one of those days

    when nothing at all
can go wrong. Across the way, I see my neighbor
lurching onto his lawn with some machine—
a rug shampooer? No, he straps a box
to his side, fastens earphones to his head,
    and walks his lawn, sweeping before him
        the sensitive disc

    of a metal detector.
What in God's name is he looking for? It is ten-thirty;
he ought to be at work. But neither am I,
so I do not hail him. Back and forth,
back and forth he trudges over the spongy grass,
    swinging the handle, his head cocked
        for a signal whose meaning

    I cannot guess. A lost
earring, perhaps, or the tap to the water meter;
no relics lie in this developed earth.
The sun moves higher overhead; he sweats,
walks on, and in my own head I begin
    to carry that heavy intentness,
        waiting for the whine

    that will let me know
I have struck—what? The cars pass on their various
errands, snapping the asphalt bubbles,
and I doze here, dreaming that something lies
under a suburban lawn, waiting to change
    my life, to draw me away from what
        I chose too long ago

to forsake it now,
on some journey out of legend, to smuggle across
the world's best-guarded borders this token,
whatever it is, that says *I have risked
my life for this moment; do not forget me.
Whatever this makes me, accept it;
by this let me be known.*

And my neighbor walks on,
hunting the emblem that will tell him who he is now
or might once have become. I will not wait
to watch him find it; let it be the lost
treasure that turns his head on the pillow
as he drifts, as I do, toward sleep,
out of the life he has chosen.

UNDERPASS

We were walking at dusk through the neighborhood
where we had fallen in love.
Just past the theater, under the railroad bridge,
we paused to watch a camper-topped pickup
negotiate the dangerous clearance there. A passenger,
a woman of maybe twenty in close-fitting jeans
and the long hair of those days, danced down
from the running board into the street and stood
where she could watch the critical, diminishing space.
She waved the driver on, and as the cab
drew abreast of where we were, we saw
another young woman crouched over the wheel,
peering first at the underside of the bridge,
then at her friend or sister, and inching slowly forward.

They were young and beautiful, we thought. And so,
to tell the truth, were we. This was probably 1964.

We held our breath as they made it through,
the passenger floated back into her seat,
and the camper's taillights melted into the traffic.
For all we knew, they were taking it a few blocks,
but something told us they had far to go.
We loaded some dreams of our own into that truck
and gripped each other's arms as it pulled away.

Today, using the phone to do some serious work
on the miles between us, we thought of them
and wondered where they had gone, with what cargo.
Like us, they're pushing fifty, or have passed it,
and may, like us, have children on one road
or another. If we could tell them anything,
we would try to thank them for having carried
some fragile promises of ours to a place
where, as things have turned out, they could be kept.
Those decades back, my love, we wished them well,
and if that wish had any force at all
they came in off the road some time ago,
and may even be as beautiful as you.

Rudolph von Abele

POET COUNTERPOET

How peaceful to have been Li-Po, lying back
drunk in a boat, without oars, among reeds,
remarking the strange truth that his arms
were clasping themselves behind his head, and
that the moon was moving in the sky: to have

been Li-Po, inventing verses, inventing verses
about Li-Po, lying back, drunk in a boat, without
oars, among reeds, at home with the moon and
with his arms, telling himself aloud that what
he made in yellow drunkenness would be revised

in blue sobriety, moon-flimmer, insects, reeds
shushing about time, his arms, the oars, the suede
surface of the river. . . . And then to be Li-Po,
or to pretend to be Li-Po, sitting upright, dead
sober, strapped into the down-screaming fiery plane,

studying the Jersey Meadows, puzzling out how
to invent verses about Li-Po, studying the Jersey
Meadows from a plane, all that lackluster broom-
grass, those sulfuric ponds, those caved-in
factories, those rusting cars craned one atop

the other, making jagged love, dead sober, and the
impossible geometry of pipes and railroad tracks,
those sour man-breaths stilling up into the regions
of the moon from dumps among the grass, among the
ponds, and to wish oneself drunkward among reeds. . . .

THE WORLD COMES GALLOPING:
A TRUE STORY

By the ruined arch, where the bougainvillea bled,
And pigeons simmered and shat in the barbaric vine
And made a noise like Plato in the barbaric vine,
He stood: old.
Old, bare feet on stone, and the serape's rose
Unfolded in the garden of his rags;
Old, and all his history hung from his severe face
As from his frame the dignity of rags.

We could not see his history, we saw
Him.
And he saw us, but could not see we stood
Huddled in our history and stuck out hand for alms.

But he could give us nothing, and asked for nothing,
Whose figure, sharp against the blue lake and violet mountains,
Was under the arch, the vine, the violent blue vulgarity of sky.
He ate a peach and wiped the pulp across his gums;
His mouth was no less ruinous than the arch.

Then at the foot of that long street,
Between the pastel stucco and the feathery pepper trees,
Horse and horseman, sudden as light, and loud,
Appeared,
And up the rise, banging the cobbles like castanets,
Lashed in their fury and fever,
Plunged:
Wall-eyed and wheezing, the lurching hammer-head,
The swaying youth, and flapping from bare heels,
The great wheel-spurs of the Conquistador.
Plunged past us, and were gone:
The crow-bait mount, the fly-bit man.

So the old one, dropping his peach-pit, spat;
Regarding the street's astonishing vacancy, said:
"Viene galopando,"—and spat again—"el mundo."

TRYING TO TELL YOU SOMETHING

To Tinkum Brooks

All things lean at you, and some are
Trying to tell you something, though of some

The heart is too full for speech. On a hill, the oak,
Immense, older than Jamestown or God, splitting

With its own weight at the great inverted
Crotch, air-spread and ice-hung, ringed with iron

Like barrel-hoops, only heavier, massive rods
Running through and bolted, and higher, the cables,

Which in summer are hidden by green leaves—the oak,
It is trying to tell you something. It wants,

In its fullness of years, to describe to you
What happens on a December night when

It stands alone in a world of snowy whiteness. The moon is full.
You can hear the stars crackle in their high brightness.

It is ten below zero, and the iron
Of hoops and reinforcement rods is continuing to contract.

There is the rhythm of a slow throb, like pain. The wind,
Northwest, is steady, and in the wind, the cables,

In a thin-honed and disinfectant purity, like
A dentist's drill, sing. They sing

Of truth, and its beauty. The oak
Wants to declare this to you, so that you

Will not be unprepared when, some December night,
You stand on a hill, in a world of whiteness, and

Stare into the crackling absoluteness of the sky. The oak
Wants to tell you because, at that moment,

In your own head, the cables will sing
With a thin-honed and disinfectant purity,

And no one can predict the consequences.

ARIZONA MIDNIGHT

The grief of the coyote seems to make
Stars quiver whiter over the blankness which
Is Arizona at midnight. In sleeping-bag,
Protected by the looped rampart of anti-rattler horsehair rope,
I take a careful twist, grinding sand on sand,
To lie on my back. I stare. Stars quiver, twitch,
In their infinite indigo. I know
Nothing to tell the stars, who go,
Age on age, along tracks they understand, and
The only answer I have for the coyote would be
My own grief, for which I have no
Tongue—indeed, scarcely understand.
Eastward, I see
No indication of dawn, not yet ready for the scream
Of inflamed distance,
Which is the significance of day.

But dimly I do see
Against that darkness, lifting in blunt agony,
The single great cactus. Once more I hear the coyote
Wail. I strain to make out the cactus. It has
Its own necessary beauty.

LAST NIGHT TRAIN

In that slick and new-fangled coach we go slam-banging
On rackety ruin of a roadbed, past caterpillar-
Green flash of last light on deserted platforms,
And I watch the other passenger at this
Late hour— a hundred and eighty pounds of
Flesh, black, female, middle-aged,
Unconsciously flung by roadbed jerks to wallow,
Unshaped, unhinged, in
A purple dress. Straps of white sandals
Are loosened to ease the bulge of color-contrasting bare instep.
Knees wide, the feet lie sidewise, sole toward sole. They
Have walked so far. Head back, flesh snores.
I wonder what she has been doing all day in N.Y.

My station at last. I look back once.
Is she missing hers? I hesitate to ask, and the snore
Is suddenly snatched into eternity.

The last red light fades into distance and darkness like
A wandering star. Where that brief roar just now was,
A last cricket is audible. That lost
Sound makes me think, with quickly suppressed
Nostalgia, of
A country lane, late night, late autumn—and there,
Alone, again I stand, part of all.
Alone, I now stand under the green station light,
Part of nothing but years.

I stare skyward at uncountable years beyond
My own little aura of pale-green light—
The complex of stars is steady in its operation.
Smell of salt sedge drifts in from seaward,
And I think of swimming, naked and seaward,
In starlight forever.

But I look up the track toward Bridgeport. I feel
Like blessing the unconscious wallow of flesh-heap
And white sandals unstrapped at bulging of instep.

I hear my heels crunch on gravel, making
My way to a parked car.

Robert Watson

THE GLASS DOOR

Was I moving through the invisible glass
    Between life and death,
When I walked through the glass door
    I thought was open?
The glass fell on me like icicles or knives,
    My clothes turned red and then my eyes.

After the nurse sponged my face the surgeon
    With needle and thread
Mended me as if I were a tattered coat.
    "You will be the same as ever
After a month on crutches and two with a cane."
    But I am not the same.

I would have sworn our sliding glass door was open,
    Nothing between in and out.
In daylight I walk as a man in darkness
    Hands out to feel
What the darkness holds, to test for walls
    That shatter,

For invisible curtains between what we see
    And what we think we see
Or rainy nights staring beyond the windshield
    Or out the kitchen window
Washing glasses in the sink. Telescopes are useless.
    Everything we cannot see is here.

PLEASE WRITE: DON'T PHONE

While there is mail there is hope.
After we have hung up I can't recall

Your words, and your voice sounds strange
Whether from distance, a bad cold, deceit
I don't know. When you call I'm asleep
Or bathing or my mouth is full of toast.

I can't think of what to say.
"We have rain"? "We have snow"?

Let us write instead: surely our fingers spread out
With pen on paper touch more of the mind's flesh
Than the sound waves moving from throat to lips
To phone, through wire, to one ear.
I can touch the paper you touch.
I can see you undressed in your calligraphy.
I can read you over and over.
I can read you day after day.
I can wait at the mailbox with my hair combed,
In my best suit.
I hang up. What did you say?
What did you say? Your phone call is gone.
I hold the envelope you addressed in my hand.
I hold the skin that covers you.

Theodore Weiss

THROUGH OUR HANDS

I see an intentness in you
as of one gazing out a window
to the far distance for something
gathering there, a face perhaps
strange as it's familiar.

At once I sense you too
are watching someone watching
in your head, like mirrors clear-
eyed in a veritable Versailles
of watching.
                    In turn I peer
through you to the next onlooker,
the next and next until I feel
I've mined them all.
                    This spot,
small as it is, but one blink
brief, the whole world wings
to through our hands clinging
to each other.
                    Stars may borrow
light more readily from remotest
kin. And waves lunge far above us,
far beyond, yet, of a single water,
cannot make a sea as uniform
as ours.
                    And because we've been
so intricately interknitted,
the lines between us drawn out
long yet taut, we're free.

Wherever the waves have ended
and the sun has set, the starlight

fettered in some far-gone time
and place,

               or in a time
and place not yet named or met,
already I, my hand through yours
outstretched, can spy those faces
blending in your face.

James Whitehead

DELTA FARMER IN A WET SUMMER

Last summer was hot and dry, a better time—
Two cuttings at the dock and two knocked up
In the fields, and a crop to fill the wagons full.
There were prime steaks and politics at night,
Gin to nine and bourbon after that—
By God, we raised some handsome bales and hell,
Then went to New Orleans as usual.

But now it rains too long, too little sun
To stop the rot. Rain beats down on the roof
At night and gives sad dreams—black bolls—
And the Thunderbird will have to go. You can smell
It on the evenings, like the smell of a filthy
Bed, or wasted borrowed money, the stink
Of a bloated dog when finally the water's down.

. . . in California they say it's dry.
They irrigate consistently, don't count
The weather in when going to the bank,
And that's damned smart, except they've got no woods
Or sloughs to crowd the fields, and dogs get killed
But rarely drown—and I think our bitch, stretched hide
And stench, contains the element of
    chance a Christian needs.

Miller Williams

THE CATERPILLAR

Today on the lip of a bowl in the backyard
we watched a caterpillar caught in the circle
of his larval assumptions

My daughter counted
half a dozen times he went around
before rolling back and laughing
I'm a caterpillar, look
she left him
measuring out his slow green way to some place
there must have been a picture of inside him

After supper
coming from putting the car up
we stopped to look
figured he crossed the yard
once every hour
and left him
when we went to bed
wrinkling no closer to my landlord's leaves
than when he somehow fell to his private circle

Later I followed
barefeet and doorclicks of my daughter
to the yard   the bowl
a milkwhite moonlight eye
in the black grass

It died

I said honey they don't live very long

In bed again
re-covered and re-kissed

she locked her arms and mumbling love to mine
until turning she slipped
into the deep bone-bottomed dish
of sleep

Stumbling drunk around the rim
I hold
the words she said to me across the dark

*I think he thought he was
going in a straight line*

A POEM FOR EMILY

Small fact and fingers and farthest one from me,
a hand's width and two generations away,
in this still present I am fifty-three.
You are not yet a full day.

When I am sixty-three, when you are ten,
and you are neither closer nor as far,
your arms will fill with what you know by then,
the arithmetic and love we do and are.

When I by blood and luck am eighty-six
and you are someplace else and thirty-three
believing in sex and god and politics
with children who look not at all like me,

sometime I know you will have read them this
so they will know I love them and say so
and love their mother. Child, whatever is
is always or never was. Long ago,

a day I watched awhile beside your bed,
I wrote this down, a thing that might be kept

awhile, to tell you what I would have said
when you were who knows what and I was dead
which is I stood and loved you while you slept.

PEOPLE

When people are born
we lift them like little heroes
as if what they have done
is a thing to be proud of.

When people die
we cover their faces
as if dying were something
to be ashamed of.

Of shameful and varied heroic things we do
except for the starting and stopping
we are never convinced
of how we feel.
We say oh, and well.

Ah, but in the beginning
and in the end.

AN AUGUST EVENING
OUTSIDE OF NASHVILLE

Seeing a chipmunk in the yard
holding a nut between its paws
while a jay in cold regard,
in a kind of punk repose,
sheds upon it what might be
contempt, for birds in Tennessee;

Following a changing cloud
while my eyelids fill with lead;
hearing the wild bees grow loud
while a wobbling, overfed
goose scolds a lazy dog
and fungus on a rotting log

makes shapes I find a message in;
when a breeze takes the sweat
barely off my bare skin,
I can almost forget
how you were with dirty feet
all tangled in my sweaty sheet.

Susan Wood

MATINEE

There's that moment in *To Catch a Thief*
when Grace Kelly surprises Cary Grant
with a kiss and we know she's in control.
She's an heiress, he's a jewel thief, but for all
her cold, imperial blondness, the sexual
belongs to her. She tells him he might see
one of the Riviera's greatest sights and she's
right, the heat in those blue eyes,
the way she drapes the long chiffon
scarf across a bosom more ample than a girl
from Main Line Philadelphia has any right to.
He never had a prayer. In 1955
she's still a year away from being
Princess Grace, a wedding my grade-school class
will watch on television, a story also
more American than we could know. The first time
I saw that movie I didn't understand,
nor why the blond-haired girl who'd never been
my friend asked me to see it after school, nor why
her father joined us there. Weren't all fathers
working weekday afternoons? In the darkened theater
he sat between us, an ordinary, gray-haired man,
his khaki work clothes streaked with oil
and grease, the rank, male sweat
of the gas station. Maybe it was that exact
moment when Grace Kelly kissed Cary Grant
he took my hand and held it
to his lap and I felt something
burrowing there, slick and blind, like the kittens
black Trouble gave birth to in a box
in our garage. I didn't move or say a word
but stared straight ahead and let him

hold me there until the final credits rolled, the way
for years afterward I stared unseeing at the world's
blank screen and let life press against me and took
whatever came. Outside the Palace Theater dusk
had fallen, night spread like a stain
across the red brick streets of my hometown, a world
grown suddenly dark and strange.

Stephen Yenser

EMBER WEEK, RESEDA

Back here the fall, spreading down the hills,
Scatters its seeds of fire through mountain ash
And gingko, the occasional pistache,
The sour gum and the purple plum alike.
Here and there a liquidambar burns
Wickedly as it turns

Its deep flame up. The fire in all things loves
The end of them. Underfoot the leaves
Crackle like crumpled letters. Even the rain,
Dripping its last at midnight from the eaves,
Pops and snaps out on the front porch steps.
Watching the logs give in

And glow, the fire like memory revise
Those other windblown trees' slow-motion blaze,
Your brush lick at a glaze of crimson lake
Somewhere in the dreamlike, liquid world
The heat's a window on, I catch myself
Again, falling awake.

Al Young

DEMEROL

The glamour of this moment too will pass.
This bright warm wind that whispers thru me now,
thru my body, a dwelling place of spirit,
will blow itself away.
                              Like laughing gas
that dentists used in 1910 for pain,
this sweet drug even now feels out-of-date.
Is it their muzak oozing from the walls,
crisp leaves of city trees quivering with rain
outside this clinic window where I lie
that make me sad & at the same time feel
that I could swim this sinking stream of joy
forever?—no how-are-you, no good-bye.

Delicious as it seems, it doesnt last.
Having to do it over & over again
means keeping up with Joneses that dont die.

THE JAMES COTTON BAND
AT KEYSTONE

And the blues, I tell you, they blew up
on target; blew the roof right off
& went whistling skyward, starward,
stilling every zooming one of us
mojo'd in the room that night, that
instant, that whenever-it-was. Torn
inside at first, we all got turned out,
twisting in a blooming space where

afternoon & evening fused like Adam
with Eve. The joyful urge to cry
mushroomed into a blinding cloudburst
of spirit wired for sound, then atomized
into one long, thunderous, cooling downpour.

What ceased to be was now & now & now.
Time somehow was what the blues froze
tight like an underground pipe before
busting it loose in glad explosions; a
blast that shattered us—ice, flow & all.
The drift of what we'd been began to
shift, dragging us neither upstream nor
down but lifting us, safe & high, above
the very storm that, only flashing moments
ago, we'd been huddling in for warmth.

Melted at last, liquefied, we became
losers to the blues & victors, both.
Now that he'd blown us away with his shout,
this reigning brownskinned wizard, wise
to the ways of alchemy, squeezed new life
back into us by breathing through cracks
in our broken hearts; coaxing & choking
while speaking in tongues that fork & bend
like the watery peripheries of time; a
crime no more punishable than what the
dreaming volcano does waking from what it was.

Believe me, the blues can be volatile too,
but the blues don't bruise; they only renew.

Chronology of LSU Press Poetry Books, 1964–1999

1964
Miller Williams, *A Circle of Stone*

1965
John William Corrington, *Lines to the South and Other Poems*

1966
Henry Taylor, *The Horse Show at Midnight*
James Whitehead, *Domains*

1967
John William Corrington and Miller Williams, eds., *Southern Writing in the Sixties: Poetry*

1968
Edgar Simmons, *Driving to Biloxi*

1969
Joyce Carol Oates, *Anonymous Sins and Other Poems*

1970
William Heyen, *Depth of Field*
Joyce Carol Oates, *Love and Its Derangements*
Stanley Plumly, *In the Outer Dark*

1971
Fred Chappell, *The World Between the Eyes*

1972
R. H. W. Dillard, *After Borges: A Sequence of New Poems*
David R. Slavitt, *Child's Play*

1973
James B. Hall, *The Hunt Within*
Joyce Carol Oates, *Angel Fire*

1974
William Mills, *Watch for the Fox*
Stanley Plumly, *Giraffe*
Dabney Stuart, *The Other Hand*

1975
Betty Adcock, *Walking Out*
Fred Chappell, *River: A Poem*

1976
Lisel Mueller, *The Private Life*

1977
Kelly Cherry, *Relativity: A Point of View*
O. B. Hardison, Jr., *Pro Musica Antiqua*
Judith Moffett, *Keeping Time*
Robert Morgan, *Land Diving*
Joyce Carol Oates, *The Fabulous Beasts*
Dabney Stuart, *Round and Round: A Triptych*
Miller Williams, *Halfway from Hoxie: New and Selected Poems*
Miller Williams, *Why God Permits Evil*

1978
Fred Chappell, *Bloodfire: A Poem*
Rosanne Coggeshall, *Hymn for Drum: A Poem*
Joyce Carol Oates, *Women Whose Lives Are Food, Men Whose Lives Are Money*
David R. Slavitt, *Rounding the Horn*

Rudolph von Abele, *A Cage for Loulou*
Marilyn Nelson Waniek, *For the Body*

1979
Jimmy Santiago Baca, *Immigrants in Our Own Land*
Fred Chappell, *Wind Mountain: A Poem*
Margaret Gibson, *Signs*
William Mills, *Stained Glass*
Richard Stansberger, *Glass Hat*
Timothy Steele, *Uncertainties and Rest*

1980
Fred Chappell, *Earthsleep: A Poem*
Wayne Dodd, *The Names You Gave It*
Robert Hershon, *The Public Hug: New and Selected Poems*
Lisel Mueller, *The Need to Hold Still*
R. M. Ryan, *Goldilocks in Later Life*
John Stone, *In All This Rain*

1981
Fred Chappell, *Midquest: A Poem*
Susan Ludvigson, *Northern Lights*
David R. Slavitt, *Dozens: A Poem*
Dave Smith, *Homage to Edgar Allan Poe*
Radcliffe Squires, *Gardens of the World*
Miller Williams, *Distractions*

1982
Margaret Gibson, *Long Walks in the Afternoon*
William Harmon, *One Long Poem*
William Hathaway, *The Gymnast of Inertia*
T. R. Hummer, *The Angelic Orders*
Dabney Stuart, *Common Ground*
Al Young, *The Blues Don't Change: New and Selected Poems*

1983
Betty Adcock, *Nettles*
James Applewhite, *Foreseeing the Journey*
Wallace Fowlie, *Characters from Proust*

Richmond Lattimore, *Continuing Conclusions: New Poems and Translations*
Anthony Petrosky, *Jurgis Petraskas*
Sean Siobhan, *Confessions of an Irish Solarnaut*
David R. Slavitt, *Big Nose*
Miller Williams, *The Boys on Their Bony Mules*

1984
Dick Allen, *Overnight in the Guest House of the Mystic*
Fred Chappell, *Castle Tzingal: A Poem*
Susan Ludvigson, *The Swimmer*
William Mills, *The Meaning of Coyotes*
Bink Noll, *The House*
Herbert Scott, *Durations*

1985
Fred Chappell, *Source*
William Hathaway, *Fish, Flesh, and Fowl*
John Stone, *Renaming the Streets*
Henry Taylor, *The Flying Change*
Marilyn Nelson Waniek, *Mama's Promises*

1986
James Applewhite, *Ode to the Chinaberry Tree and Other Poems*
Margaret Gibson, *Memories of the Future: The Daybooks of Tina Modotti*
Susan Ludvigson, *The Beautiful Noon of No Shadow*
Lisel Mueller, *Second Language*
Bin Ramke, *The Language Student*
David R. Slavitt, *The Walls of Thebes*
Miller Williams, *Imperfect Love*

1987
Dick Allen, *Flight and Pursuit*
Martha McFerren, *Contours for Ritual*
Julia Randall, *Moving in Memory*
Dabney Stuart, *Don't Look Back*

1988
Betty Adcock, *Beholdings*
Kelly Cherry, *Natural Theology*
Daniel Hoffman, *Hang-Gliding from Helicon: New and Selected Poems, 1948–1988*

Elizabeth Seydel Morgan, *Parties*
John Stone, *The Smell of Matches*

1989
James Applewhite, *Lessons in Soaring*
Fred Chappell, *First and Last Words*
Brendan Galvin, *Wampanoag Traveler: Being, in Letters, the Life and Times of Loranzo Newcomb, American and Natural Historian: A Poem*
Margaret Gibson, *Out in the Open*
Lisel Mueller, *Waving from Shore*
David R. Slavitt, *Equinox and Other Poems*
Miller Williams, *Living on the Surface: New and Selected Poems*

1990
Catharine Savage Brosman, *Journeying from Canyon de Chelly*
Susan Ludvigson, *To Find the Gold*
David R. Slavitt, *Eight Longer Poems*
Dabney Stuart, *Narcissus Dreaming*
Marilyn Nelson Waniek, *The Homeplace*

1991
Cathryn Hankla, *Afterimages*
Pinkie Gordon Lane, *Girl at the Window*
David Middleton, *The Burning Fields*
Carole Simmons Oles, *The Deed*
Gibbons Ruark, *Rescue the Perishing*
Susan Wood, *Campo Santo*

1992
Kathryn Stripling Byer, *Wildwood Flower*
Greg Delanty, *Southward*
Brendan Galvin, *Saints in Their Ox-Hide Boat: A Poem*
Robert Hazel, *Clock of Clay: New and Selected Poems*
Deborah Pope, *Fanatic Heart*
Julia Randall, *The Path to Fairview: New and Selected Poems*
Henry Taylor, *The Horseshow at Midnight* and *An Afternoon of Pocket Billiards* (single-volume reissue)

1993
James Applewhite, *A History of the River*
Fred Chappell, *C*
Kelly Cherry, *God's Loud Hand*
Margaret Gibson, *The Vigil: A Poem in Four Voices*
Susan Ludvigson, *Everything Winged Must Be Dreaming*
Elizabeth Seydel Morgan, *The Governor of Desire*
Stephen Yenser, *The Fire in All Things*

1994
Alison Hawthorne Deming, *Science and Other Poems*
R. H. W. Dillard, *Just Here, Just Now*
Anthony Petrosky, *Red and Yellow Boat*
David R. Slavitt, *Crossroads*
Dabney Stuart, *Light Years: New and Selected Poems*
Marilyn Nelson Waniek, *Magnificat*
Theodore Weiss, *A Sum of Destructions*

1995
Betty Adcock, *The Difficult Wheel*
Fred Chappell, *Spring Garden: New and Selected Poems*
Jane Gentry, *A Garden in Kentucky*
Daniel Hoffman, *Middens of the Tribe: A Poem*
Deborah Pope, *Mortal World*
Jan Richman, *Because the Brain Can Be Talked into Anything*
Paulette Roeske, *Divine Attention*
Dave Smith, *Fate's Kite: Poems, 1991–1995*
Robert Watson, *The Pendulum: New and Selected Poems*

1996
Catharine Savage Brosman, *Passages*
Nicole Cooley, *Resurrection*
Brendan Galvin, *Sky and Island Light*
T. R. Hummer, *Walt Whitman in Hell*
Susan Ludvigson, *Trinity*
Lisel Mueller, *Alive Together: New and Selected Poems*
James Seay, *Open Field, Understory: New and Selected Poems*
David R. Slavitt, *A Gift: The Life of da Ponte: A Poem*
R. T. Smith, *Trespasser*

Dabney Stuart, *Long Gone*
Henry Taylor, *Understanding Fiction: Poems, 1986–1996*

1997
Claudia Emerson Andrews, *Pharaoh, Pharaoh*
James Applewhite, *Daytime and Starlight*
Kelly Cherry, *Death and Transfiguration*
James Harmon Clinton, *What Is Fair*
Joshua Clover, *madonna anno domini*
Alison Hawthorne Deming, *The Monarchs: A Poem Sequence*
Reginald Gibbons, *Sparrow: New and Selected Poems*
Margaret Gibson, *Earth Elegy: New and Selected Poems*
Cathryn Hankla, *Negative History*
Marilyn Nelson, *The Fields of Praise: New and Selected Poems*
Brenda Marie Osbey, *All Saints: New and Selected Poems*
David R. Slavitt, *Epic and Epigram: Two Elizabethan Entertainments*

1998
Gerald Barrax, *From a Person Sitting in Darkness: New and Selected Poems*
Ben Belitt, *This Scribe, My Hand: The Complete Poems of Ben Belitt*
Paula Closson Buck, *The Acquiescent Villa*
Kathryn Stripling Byer, *Black Shawl*
Stephen Cushman, *Blue Pajamas*
Kate Daniels, *Four Testimonies*
Ann B. Dobie, ed., *Uncommonplace: An Anthology of Contemporary Louisiana Poets*
George Garrett, *Days of Our Lives Lie in Fragments: New and Old Poems, 1957–1997*
Elizabeth Seydel Morgan, *On Long Mountain*
Lisel Mueller, *Dependencies* (reissue)
Barbara Ras, *Bite Every Sorrow*
Stephen Sandy, *The Thread: New and Selected Poems*
Seven American Poets, *A New Pléiade: Selected Poems*
John Stone, *Where Water Begins: New Poems and Prose*
Robert Penn Warren, *The Collected Poems of Robert Penn Warren,* edited by John Burt

1999
Roland Flint, *Easy*
Brendan Galvin, *The Strength of a Named Thing*

Conrad Hilberry, *Player Piano*
David Huddle, *Summer Lake: New and Selected Poems*
Jan Heller Levi, *Once I Gazed at You in Wonder*
David Middleton, *Beyond the Chandeleurs*
Sue Owen, *My Doomsday Sampler*
Deborah Pope, *Falling Out of the Sky*
Gibbons Ruark, *Passing Through Customs: New and Selected Poems*
Stephen Sandy, *Black Box*
Dabney Stuart, *Settlers*
Eleanor Ross Taylor, *Late Leisure*

LSU Press Poetry Books by Author, 1964–1999

Betty Adcock
>*Walking Out* (1975)
>*Nettles* (1983)
>*Beholdings* (1988)
>*The Difficult Wheel* (1995)

Dick Allen
>*Overnight in the Guest House of the Mystic* (1984)
>*Flight and Pursuit* (1987)

Claudia Emerson Andrews
>*Pharaoh, Pharaoh* (1997)

James Applewhite
>*Foreseeing the Journey* (1983)
>*Ode to the Chinaberry Tree and Other Poems* (1986)
>*Lessons in Soaring* (1989)
>*A History of the River* (1993)
>*Daytime and Starlight* (1997)

Jimmy Santiago Baca
>*Immigrants in Our Own Land* (1979)

Gerald Barrax
>*From a Person Sitting in Darkness: New and Selected Poems* (1998)

Ben Belitt
>*This Scribe, My Hand: The Complete Poems of Ben Belitt* (1998)

Catharine Savage Brosman
> *Journeying from Canyon de Chelly* (1990)
> *Passages* (1996)

Paula Closson Buck
> *The Acquiescent Villa* (1998)

Kathryn Stripling Byer
> *Wildwood Flower* (1992)
> *Black Shawl* (1998)

Fred Chappell
> *The World Between the Eyes* (1971)
> *River: A Poem* (1975)
> *Bloodfire: A Poem* (1978)
> *Wind Mountain: A Poem* (1979)
> *Earthsleep: A Poem* (1980)
> *Midquest: A Poem* (1981)
> *Castle Tzingal: A Poem* (1984)
> *Source* (1985)
> *First and Last Words* (1989)
> *C* (1993)
> *Spring Garden: New and Selected Poems* (1995)

Kelly Cherry
> *Relativity: A Point of View* (1977)
> *Natural Theology* (1988)
> *God's Loud Hand* (1993)
> *Death and Transfiguration* (1997)

James Harmon Clinton
> *What Is Fair* (1997)

Joshua Clover
> *madonna anno domini* (1997)

Rosanne Coggeshall
> *Hymn for Drum: A Poem* (1978)

Nicole Cooley
> *Resurrection* (1996)

John William Corrington
>>> *Lines to the South and Other Poems* (1965)
>>> *Southern Writing in the Sixties: Poetry* (1967; coedited, with Miller Williams)

Stephen Cushman
>>> *Blue Pajamas* (1998)

Kate Daniels
>>> *Four Testimonies* (1998)

Greg Delanty
>>> *Southward* (1992)

Alison Hawthorne Deming
>>> *Science and Other Poems* (1994)
>>> *The Monarchs: A Poem Sequence* (1997)

R. H. W. Dillard
>>> *After Borges: A Sequence of New Poems* (1972)
>>> *Just Here, Just Now* (1994)

Ann B. Dobie, editor
>>> *Uncommonplace: An Anthology of Contemporary Louisiana Poets* (1998)

Wayne Dodd
>>> *The Names You Gave It* (1980)

Roland Flint
>>> *Easy* (1999)

Wallace Fowlie
>>> *Characters from Proust* (1983)

Brendan Galvin
>>> *Wampanoag Traveler: Being, in Letters, the Life and Times of Loranzo Newcomb,*
>>> *American and Natural Historian: A Poem* (1989)
>>> *Saints in Their Ox-Hide Boat: A Poem* (1992)
>>> *Sky and Island Light* (1996)
>>> *The Strength of a Named Thing* (1999)

George Garrett
>>> *Days of Our Lives Lie in Fragments: New and Old Poems, 1957–1997* (1998)

Jane Gentry
> *A Garden in Kentucky* (1995)

Reginald Gibbons
> *Sparrow: New and Selected Poems* (1997)

Margaret Gibson
> *Signs* (1979)
> *Long Walks in the Afternoon* (1982)
> *Memories of the Future: The Daybooks of Tina Modotti* (1986)
> *Out in the Open* (1989)
> *The Vigil: A Poem in Four Voices* (1993)
> *Earth Elegy: New and Selected Poems* (1997)

James B. Hall
> *The Hunt Within* (1973)

Cathryn Hankla
> *Afterimages* (1991)
> *Negative History* (1997)

O. B. Hardison, Jr.
> *Pro Musica Antiqua* (1977)

William Harmon
> *One Long Poem* (1982)

William Hathaway
> *The Gymnast of Inertia* (1982)
> *Fish, Flesh, and Fowl* (1985)

Robert Hazel
> *Clock of Clay: New and Selected Poems* (1992)

Robert Hershon
> *The Public Hug: New and Selected Poems* (1980)

William Heyen
> *Depth of Field* (1970)

Conrad Hilberry
> *Player Piano* (1999)

Daniel Hoffman

    Hang-Gliding from Helicon: New and Selected Poems, 1948–1988 (1988)

    Middens of the Tribe: A Poem (1995)

David Huddle

    Summer Lake: New and Selected Poems (1999)

T. R. Hummer

    The Angelic Orders (1982)

    Walt Whitman in Hell (1996)

Pinkie Gordon Lane

    Girl at the Window (1991)

Richmond Lattimore

    Continuing Conclusions: New Poems and Translations (1983)

Jan Heller Levi

    Once I Gazed at You in Wonder (1999)

Susan Ludvigson

    Northern Lights (1981)

    The Swimmer (1984)

    The Beautiful Noon of No Shadow (1986)

    To Find the Gold (1990)

    Everything Winged Must Be Dreaming (1993)

    Trinity (1996)

Martha McFerren

    Contours for Ritual (1987)

David Middleton

    The Burning Fields (1991)

    Beyond the Chandeleurs (1999)

William Mills

    Watch for the Fox (1974)

    Stained Glass (1979)

    The Meaning of Coyotes (1984)

Judith Moffett

    Keeping Time (1977)

Elizabeth Seydel Morgan
> *Parties* (1988)
> *The Governor of Desire* (1993)
> *On Long Mountain* (1998)

Robert Morgan
> *Land Diving* (1977)

Lisel Mueller
> *The Private Life* (1976)
> *The Need to Hold Still* (1980)
> *Second Language* (1986)
> *Waving from Shore* (1989)
> *Alive Together: New and Selected Poems* (1996)
> *Dependencies* (1998; reissue)

Marilyn Nelson (*see also* Marilyn Nelson Waniek)
> *The Fields of Praise: New and Selected Poems* (1997)

Bink Noll
> *The House* (1984)

Joyce Carol Oates
> *Anonymous Sins and Other Poems* (1969)
> *Love and Its Derangements* (1970)
> *Angel Fire* (1973)
> *The Fabulous Beasts* (1977)
> *Women Whose Lives Are Food, Men Whose Lives Are Money* (1978)

Carole Simmons Oles
> *The Deed* (1991)

Brenda Marie Osbey
> *All Saints: New and Selected Poems* (1997)

Sue Owen
> *My Doomsday Sampler* (1999)

Anthony Petrosky
> *Jurgis Petraskas* (1983)
> *Red and Yellow Boat* (1994)

Stanley Plumly

> *In the Outer Dark* (1970)
> *Giraffe* (1974)

Deborah Pope

> *Fanatic Heart* (1992)
> *Mortal World* (1995)
> *Falling Out of the Sky* (1999)

Bin Ramke

> *The Language Student* (1986)

Julia Randall

> *Moving in Memory* (1987)
> *The Path to Fairview* (1992)

Barbara Ras

> *Bite Every Sorrow* (1998)

Jan Richman

> *Because the Brain Can Be Talked into Anything* (1995)

Paulette Roeske

> *Divine Attention* (1995)

Gibbons Ruark

> *Rescue the Perishing* (1991)
> *Passing Through Customs: New and Selected Poems* (1999)

R. M. Ryan

> *Goldilocks in Later Life* (1980)

Stephen Sandy

> *The Thread: New and Selected Poems* (1998)
> *Black Box* (1999)

Herbert Scott

> *Durations* (1984)

James Seay

> *Open Field, Understory: New and Selected Poems* (1996)

Seven American Poets
>*A New Pléiade: Selected Poems* (1998)

Edgar Simmons
>*Driving to Biloxi* (1968)

Sean Siobhan
>*Confessions of an Irish Solarnaut* (1983)

David R. Slavitt
>*Child's Play* (1972)
>*Rounding the Horn* (1978)
>*Dozens: A Poem* (1981)
>*Big Nose* (1983)
>*The Walls of Thebes* (1986)
>*Equinox and Other Poems* (1989)
>*Eight Longer Poems* (1990)
>*Crossroads* (1994)
>*A Gift: The Life of da Ponte: A Poem* (1996)
>*Epic and Epigram: Two Elizabethan Entertainments* (1997)
>*PS3569.L3* (1998)

Dave Smith
>*Homage to Edgar Allan Poe* (1981)
>*Fate's Kite: Poems, 1991–1995* (1995)

R. T. Smith
>*Trespasser* (1996)

Radcliffe Squires
>*Gardens of the World* (1981)

Richard Stansberger
>*Glass Hat* (1979)

Timothy Steele
>*Uncertainties and Rest* (1979)

John Stone
>*In All This Rain* (1980)
>*Renaming the Streets* (1985)
>*The Smell of Matches* (1988)
>*Where Water Begins: New Poems and Prose* (1998)

Dabney Stuart

    The Other Hand (1974)

    Round and Round: A Triptych (1977)

    Common Ground (1982)

    Don't Look Back (1987)

    Narcissus Dreaming (1990)

    Light Years: New and Selected Poems (1994)

    Long Gone (1996)

    Settlers (1999)

Eleanor Ross Taylor

    Late Leisure (1999)

Henry Taylor

    The Horse Show at Midnight (1966)

    The Flying Change (1985)

    The Horse Show at Midnight and *An Afternoon of Pocket Billiards* (1992; single-
       volume reissue)

    Understanding Fiction: Poems, 1986–1996 (1996)

Rudolphe von Abele

    A Cage for Loulou (1978)

Marilyn Nelson Waniek (*see also* Marilyn Nelson)

    For the Body (1978)

    Mama's Promises (1985)

    The Homeplace (1990)

    Magnificat (1994)

Robert Penn Warren

    The Collected Poems of Robert Penn Warren, edited by John Burt (1998)

Robert Watson

    The Pendulum: New and Selected Poems (1995)

Theodore Weiss

    A Sum of Destructions (1994)

James Whitehead

    Domains (1966)

Miller Williams

 A Circle of Stone (1964)

 Southern Writing in the Sixties: Poetry (1967; coedited, with John William Cor-
  rington)

 Halfway from Hoxie: New and Selected Poems (1977)

 Why God Permits Evil (1977)

 Distractions (1981)

 The Boys on Their Bony Mules (1983)

 Imperfect Love (1986)

 Living on the Surface: New and Selected Poems (1989)

Susan Wood

 Campo Santo (1991)

Stephen Yenser

 The Fire in All Things (1993)

Al Young

 The Blues Don't Change: New and Selected Poems (1982)